50 Ways to Love Your Stepchild

Approaching the Heart with a Rational Mind

Sarah Cline, Ph.D.

Copyright © 2023 Sarah Cline, Ph.D.
All rights reserved.

The contents of this book may not be reproduced, duplicated, or transmitted without direct written permission from the author.

Under no circumstances will any legal responsibility or blame be held against the publisher for any reparation, damages, or monetary loss due to the information herein, either directly or indirectly.

Legal Notice

This book is copyright-protected. This is only for personal use. You cannot amend, distribute, sell, use, quote, or paraphrase any part of the content within this book without the consent of the author.

Disclaimer Notice

Please note the information contained within this document is for educational and entertainment purposes only. Every attempt has been made to provide accurate, up-to-date, and reliable complete information. No warranties of any kind are expressed or implied. Readers acknowledge that the author is not engaging in the rendering of legal, financial, medical, or professional advice. The content of this book has been derived from various sources. Please consult a licensed professional before attempting any techniques outlined in this book.

By reading this document, the reader agrees that under no circumstances is the author responsible for any losses, direct or indirect, which are incurred as a result of the use of the information contained within this document, including, but not limited to, errors, omissions, or inaccuracies.

Contents

Introduction   1

1. Understanding Personality Types: a Deep Dive   4
2. Communication Is Always Key   19
3. Emotional Closeness   34
4. Navigating Social Needs   47
5. Balance a Happy Family Dynamic   60
6. Establishing Healthy Boundaries   74
7. Have Fun   84
8. Final Thoughts   107

Appendices   119

Introduction

Hey there, and welcome to *50 Ways to Love Your Stepchild*. If you have found yourself flipping through these pages, chances are you've recently tied the knot with someone who already has a child or children. Firstly, congratulations on forging that special union and finding your forever someone. Secondly, kudos to you for making the effort to build a solid connection with your stepchild. You have already begun the hard work just by starting this book.

Within the pages of this comprehensive series, we'll delve into three archetypal personas: the introspective Cave Dweller (CD), the expressive Mountain Yeller (MY), and the versatile Straddler, which embodies a fusion of traits. Recognizing and comprehending these archetypes is essential as they intricately shape the dynamics of all relationships. Our objective is to provide you with an arsenal of skills with which to fortify your connections with others as well as yourself. Moreover, as you gain insight into yourself, you become a more valuable presence for others—certainly including your stepchild.

Empowered by the wisdom found in this guide, you'll not only interpret actions but also discern the underlying motivations behind them with heightened ease. Get ready to see your stepchild—and perhaps yourself—in an entirely new and enlightening perspective.

The Influence of Individualities

In the chapters ahead, we'll demystify the core attributes of CDs, MYs, and Straddlers, celebrating the intricacies of each type. It is in grasping these distinctions that you will accurately interpret your stepchild's behaviors within the unique contexts of their personality, sidestepping assumptions that often lead to toxic environments and unneeded arguments.

Frequently in relationships, conflicts and misunderstandings are wrongly attributed to a deficit of love, empathy, or respect. More often than not, however, it's all a matter of understanding. When we fail to recognize the inherent personality traits steering our stepchild's actions, we risk misinterpreting their intentions, which leads to unnecessary tension. It's not always about agreement or shared perspectives; it's about acknowledging and respecting these inherent differences. By acknowledging the fundamental personality traits of CDs, MYs, and Straddlers, we may cultivate greater empathy for our stepchildren, allowing love to blossom in its entirety and creating an enduring relationship that will last a lifetime.

Preliminary Considerations

Like other volumes in this series, *50 Ways to Love Your Stepchild* doesn't promise quick fixes. Instead, it underscores "love" as an active pursuit demanding both attention and effort. While you'll discover a wealth of guidance here, the authentic application of these insights rests in your hands. Love is work.

Engaging with this material also necessitates introspection. There will be moments challenging your current understanding of parenting and relationships and indeed of life itself. It's precisely in these moments that genuine growth occurs. The rewards of your efforts could hardly be sweeter—a true incentive.

So, welcome to the journey. Embrace your own growth, and connect with your stepchild on a more profound and meaningful level. There is no better way to deepen the bond with your spouse than by cultivating an enduring bond with your child. Through patience and hard work, you're not merely enhancing a single bond but refining how you connect, live, and share your essence.

Chapter One

Understanding Personality Types: a Deep Dive

Do you find yourself needing help understanding your stepchild's personality traits? Are you frustrated that they're so dissimilar to yours?

Understanding personality types is an essential piece of the puzzle when seeking to understand your stepchild. Appreciating them means discovering their true layers and complexities, and all of them should garner your attention if you are ever to experience a happy and healthy relationship with them and your spouse.

In this chapter, we will discuss the personality types of the Cave Dweller stepchild, which we will refer to as CD, the Mountain Yeller stepchild, or MY, and the Straddler stepchild. Learning about these three basic personality types will give you a clearer picture of the unique benefits and challenges each creates. And understanding that is an essential first step to bringing harmony and happiness into your everyday life.

Origins of Personality Types

Before the modern-day classifications of CDs and MYs, and even before psychiatrists and psychologists stepped onto the scene, ancient civilizations sought to explain human behavior and its various nuances.

The Ancient Greeks

The ancient Greeks developed the theory of "four humors" to explain the causes of both mental and physical health and illness. This theory suggested that an individual's temperament was influenced by bodily fluids: blood (sanguine), yellow bile (choleric), black bile (melancholic), and phlegm (phlegmatic). The Greeks thought these humors were directly related to being sanguine (cheerful), choleric (short-tempered), melancholic (reserved), or phlegmatic (relaxed). Therefore, the balance of these humors was believed to influence an individual's temperament, health, and overall disposition. An imbalance in these humors led to behaviors that today we associate with certain mental illnesses. For example:

Sanguine (blood) was associated with cheerful, optimistic, enthusiastic personality traits. An imbalance was thought to be due to a person having too much blood in their body, which would cause them to be overly confident and have impulsive behavior. Possible narcissistic and bipolar disorder.

Choleric (yellow bile) was associated with being ambitious, passionate, and easily angered. It was thought that an imbalance would cause anger, irritability, or extremely aggressive behavior and rage. Possible borderline personality disorder.

Melancholic (black bile) was associated with being thoughtful, reflective, and often sad or depressed. This imbalance was associated with melancholy and depression.

Phlegmatic (phlegm) was associated with being calm, reliable, and often unemotional or apathetic. An imbalance was associated with lethargy, sluggishness, or a lack of motivation, which, much like melancholic, is a symptom of depression.

Treating these emotional ailments is where things got even more interesting. If the Greeks thought you had an imbalance of any of these four humors, your stepchild would likely have received one of the following treatments:

Dietary Changes: Prescribed depending on the humor in excess. For instance, someone deemed overly choleric might be advised to avoid hot or spicy foods that would "agitate" the yellow bile.

Bloodletting: If your stepchild were someone believed to have an excess of sanguine humor, it was common practice to prescribe bloodletting. This process involved removing blood from the body by way of leeches or actual cutting.

Purging: To remove excess bile or phlegm, laxatives were used, as were emetics, which induced vomiting.

Baths/Sweating: To promote toxin removal, balms and ointments were applied to the skin to help imbalance these four humors.

The Greeks' attempts to "treat" imbalances in personality or health were based on the observations and the knowledge they had at the time. The four humors theory was eventually replaced with more accurate medical models, but its influence can still be seen in some of our languages today.

The Introvert and the Extrovert

Carl Gustav Jung (1875–1961) was a Swiss psychiatrist, psychoanalyst, and the father of analytical psychology. He developed several concepts that had a profound influence on both psychology and popular culture. One of his most notable contributions was the concept of "introversion" and "extraversion" (often used in the more modern manner: introvert and extrovert). Jung's theory asserts that introversion and extraversion are attitudes that represent the direction in which a person's psychic energy flows.

Extraversion (Extrovert)

According to Jung, the extrovert's energy flows outward. This personality type is more oriented toward the external world and derives energy from interacting with its surroundings, including people, events, and situations. If your stepchild is an extrovert, they tend to be more outgoing, social, and interested in external events. They are typically action-oriented and more comfortable in social situations than an introverted parent. External factors influence extroverts, who are occasionally prone to negative introspection.

Introversion (Introvert)

As the name suggests, the introvert's energy flows inward. This personality type is more oriented toward the internal world, relying on introspection and internal reflection. If your stepchild is introverted, they are generally more reserved and often feel more comfortable with individual activities or smaller group settings. They derive energy and pleasure from thinking, daydreaming, or exploring ideas. Although an introverted person's daily practices tend to lead to social isolation, they tend to have a small number of deep connections with people of their choosing.

Jung believed that everyone has an introverted and extroverted side, with one being more dominant than the other. It's a spectrum, and while some people might be near the extremes of that spectrum, most individuals lie somewhere in between.

Cave Dweller (CD) and Mountain Yeller (MY)

While not strictly rooted in these historical contexts, the CD and MY classifications are evolved constructs reflecting the human desire to understand ourselves and others in our world more deeply.

While our contemporary understanding of the CD and MY classifications doesn't stem directly from ancient Greek or Jungian theories, much like their historical counterparts, they are observed patterns in modern relationships. By identifying recurring patterns, we can forge tools to help us navigate and harmonize interpersonal interactions.

Deeper Dive into the Cave Dweller (CD)

We must first learn about their traits to determine whether you and your stepchild fall into the CD or MY category.

Reserved Nature

If your stepchild is a CD, they will be predominantly calm and reserved. CDs are introspective and tend to hold their emotions close to their chest because they value their inner world and the sanctuary it provides. Their reserved nature doesn't mean that they are indifferent or don't care about those around them; it just means that they process their emotions internally and over time.

For instance, after an argument, a CD might withdraw to process their feelings rather than immediately confront an issue. A CD does this because they typically feel uncomfortable with strife and need time to work through their emotions and how to communicate their feelings.

Socially, a CD is often found in quieter corners engaging in deep conversation with one or two individuals rather than in the center of a party. In group discussions, a CD will offer insights only if specifically asked or if they feel strongly about a topic.

Logical Thinking and Literal Communication

A CD leans more toward analytical and logical thinking. They make decisions only after careful contemplation and weighing the pros and cons. They work hard to keep their emotions from clouding their judgment. This logical thinking manifests in their communication; they will get to the point without inserting emotions or using stories to embellish their point.

For example, if you discuss a film with a CD, they will likely dissect plot points with impeccable logic and even point out strengths and weaknesses, but they often miss the emotional undertones of the movie. If you ask a CD if they liked the cake you brought for dessert, they might reply, "Yes," without diving into flowery descriptives.

It's important to note that a CD may also get frustrated with an embellished story that takes longer to get to the point. It doesn't mean they don't want to hear the story or don't care what you have to say; their brain is just geared toward immediate outcomes.

Need for Space

A CD has an inherent need for emotional and physical personal space. For them, requiring space is not about distancing themselves from loved ones. It's about needing solitude to recharge and reflect.

CDs enjoy reading books in a cozy nook or going for solitary walks. They may listen to music while cooking dinner instead of talking. This alone time is essential for a CD, especially after a day filled with social interactions.

Singular Focus

A CD has unparalleled concentration when engrossed in a task and prefers completing that task to their satisfaction before tackling another.

If you attempt to talk to a CD while they're writing an email, for example, they may be so absorbed in what they're writing that you'll be tuned out. It's not that what you're saying is unimportant to them; it's just challenging for them to spread their focus on more than one thing at a time because they give each item their full attention.

Social Preferences

Traditionally, if your stepchild is labeled an introvert, others would consider them anti-social. But that couldn't be farther from the truth. An introvert, or a CD, just leans toward more intimate social interactions. Large gatherings can overwhelm a CD and drain their mental and emotional battery.

Emotional Processing

While CDs might not outwardly express their emotions, they experience them deeply. However, their internal reflections may lead to a delay in their outward emotional expression. While a CD may seem distant after an emotional confrontation, they must process the interaction before reacting. A CD needs time to contemplate a disagreement, analyze the conversation, and figure out where things went wrong before they can move on to a resolution. This meditation is essential for a CD's family member to understand; the more you push them to express themselves, the more they will clam up in response.

Deeper Dive into the Mountain Yeller (MY)

If your stepchild is an extrovert, chances are they've been called that more than once in their lifetime. An extrovert is typically known for being outgoing and the life of any party. But there's so much more to them than meets the eye.

Outgoing Nature/Group Socialization

An MY is inherently outgoing. Their energy thrives on interactions and being around people as often as possible. Instead of needing time alone to recharge, MYs wants to be out and involved.

At a social event, MYs will be the first to initiate games and dancing and will often bounce from person to person, catching up rather than focusing on one task at a time. Deep conversations are still on the table, but not at a social event. An MY usually rallies their friends for a group outing over a weekend rather than sitting at home reading a book or watching TV. Even in the workplace, MYs love group projects and find collaborative brainstorming and teamwork exciting.

Emotion-Driven

MYs are heart-ruled because they lead with their intuition and emotions. Being ruled by their heart doesn't mean their decisions are devoid of logic, but their feelings heavily influence their reactions. MYs can be emotional during arguments but are also the first to send a heartfelt message to a friend or family member upon hearing they are having a rough time.

An MY's emotions will show throughout their storytelling, so be patient when they tell you about an event or relay the plot to a movie. Chances are both will be full of details and embellishments.

Connection and Touch

MYs crave genuine connections and physical touch, whether it's a hug, a pat on the back, or simply holding hands. It reinforces their feeling of being connected. In relating with you, an MY will crave physical affection and see it as a top priority over other needs—something we'll discuss in depth a bit later.

Dynamic Focus

An MY is a natural multitasker. Instead of focusing on one task at a time, their attention shifts between assignments. They enjoy the energy they get from juggling multiple things and often get bored working on one project for an extended period.

An MY doesn't mind dealing with paperwork but works through it while watching television or listening to music. As for conversations, an MY loves to chat, but don't be surprised if you find them scrolling on their phone while talking with you. It's not that they think what you have to say is unimportant; their mind simply runs at a faster rate than a CD's, making them more comfortable processing more than one thing at a time.

Inferential Communication

An MY often communicates using stories, anecdotes, and metaphors rather than getting straight to the point. They rely on indirect implications and expect others to infer meanings, which can confuse some who aren't familiar with their communication style.

During an argument, someone may find it hard to decipher what the MY really wants, even if they feel they have expressed those needs directly. It's essential to have a middle ground where communication is concerned, especially if your parent is an MY and you are a CD, because the communication styles between personalities are very different.

Immediate Emotional Expression

Unlike their CD counterparts, MYs are quick to express their emotions. They're an open book and rarely hesitate to share their feelings of joy and disappointment. This can be overwhelming for a CD uncomfortable with an emotional display.

One of the greatest fears an MY faces is the fear of rejection. If an MY has a CD stepparent who usually pulls away at any sign of conflict, this can be a bone of contention. An MY will take a CD stepparent's withdrawal as a sign of personal rejection. If you are a CD with an MY stepchild, it's important to communicate that you are not rejecting them and need time to wrap your head around and process the disagreement. Give the MY verbal and physical affirmations whenever possible.

If you are a CD and your stepchild is an MY, don't panic; it doesn't mean you cannot have a successful stepparent/stepchild relationship. There are plenty of amazing and fulfilling relationships between opposites. It just means it will take time, work, and patience to learn one another's needs and effectively communicate.

The Straddler

If your stepchild is a Straddler, they are adaptable and enjoy the best of both worlds. They can immerse themselves in a book like a CD or be the life of a party like an MY. They possess an emotional agility that allows them to straddle their personality types seamlessly. While this book predominantly focuses on CD and MY personality types, Straddlers can use it to understand the extremes and navigate their middle ground more effectively.

Excellent Balance Between Reflection and Expression

A Straddler can introspect like a CD, valuing quiet moments of thought. Yet, they also appreciate the expressive vitality that an MY has and share their feelings and ideas openly when a situation calls for it. They are as happy spending a quiet evening reading or attending a book club as they are actively participating in a lively discussion.

Adaptable in Social Situations

While they might not always be the life of the party, Straddlers easily adjust to situations based on the social settings and the company involved. They can engage in a one-on-one conversation at a party and then join a group game or be at the party's center later in the evening.

Values: Both Logic and Emotion

A Straddler approaches situations with a logical mindset but is equally attuned to emotional undercurrents. They value the importance of feelings in decision-making. For example, if a colleague faces a personal issue, the Straddler will offer practical solutions while providing emotional support.

Flexibility in Needs and Fears

The Straddler's hierarchy of needs will fluctuate based on circumstances, and they might experience the same fears as a CD, such as loss of security, as well as the MY's fear of rejection. However, adaptability allows them to prioritize different aspects of their life. While working on an important business project, they will prioritize career stability, but in downtime, they will focus on relationships and personal connections.

Fluid Communication Styles

A Straddler can communicate directly and inferentially, often adjusting communication based on the recipient. For example, when conversing with an analytical boss, they will be direct and to the point, but when they talk to their best friend, they become expressive and delve into all the nitty-gritty details.

Straddlers possess an innate ability to mediate and find common ground, especially in relationships where CDs and MYs might find themselves at odds. Their adaptability enables them to comprehend and empathize with both personality types, easing communication and diminishing misunderstandings.

A Straddler may seem like the perfect personality type. However, everyone encounters their share of struggles. The flexibility of a Straddler can confuse preferences and needs. The Straddler might sometimes feel stretched or trapped in the middle, particularly in a polarized situation where they wish to please others so much that they struggle to voice their disagreements. A Straddler must discern what is truly significant to them while learning to navigate others' personality types, much like everyone else.

So, How Do You Find Common Ground?

"I'm a CD, and my stepchild is an MY; is my relationship with them doomed?"

No! In this book, we don't tell you how to "cope" with differences. We allow you to realize each person's unique strengths in a relationship. A CD's introspection can balance an MY's spontaneity. An MY's vivacity and exuberance can harmonize beautifully with a CD's depth and stability.

Recognizing these different traits is merely the first step to a healthy relationship. The real challenge, and indeed the focus of this book, is to find ways to navigate the complexities of these interactions. After all, the beauty of a relationship truly unfolds in the dance between these personalities.

Key Takeaways

Diving into the intricacies of personality types isn't about affixing labels but enriching our understanding. With these insights, you're now armed with the necessary vocabulary to navigate the labyrinth of human emotions and connections, fostering an environment where love thrives, understanding blossoms, and relationships flourish. As we traverse this journey, let's remember that the goal isn't to change either person but to adapt, understand, and love more deeply.

The foundation for a nurturing relationship starts with understanding—understanding yourself, your stepchild, and the dynamics of your interaction. With the knowledge of CD and MY personality traits, you're well on your way to deepening that understanding, setting the stage for the subsequent chapters that will guide you to cherish your stepchild in ways that resonate with all of you.

Understanding personality differences is essential for nurturing compatibility. This chapter has illuminated the fundamental traits of CDs, MYs, and Straddlers.

- **Reserved Nature:** Respect your CD stepchild's need for personal space and quiet reflection. Don't force immediate emotional reactions.

- **Logical Thinking:** Recognize your CD stepchild's analytical approach. Be patient as they process before expressing feelings.

- **Singular Focus:** Acknowledge that multitasking is difficult for your CD stepchild. Allow them to complete or pause their task before they give you their full attention.

- **Emotion-Driven:** Empathize with your MY stepchild's emotions. Give them positive affirmations/compliments and physical affection.

- **Inferential Communication:** Listen for meanings implied indirectly in your MY stepchild's stories. Learn to read between the lines.

- **Dynamic Focus:** Accept your MY stepchild's wandering attention. Multitasking is in their nature. However, if you need their full focus, tell them.

- **Excellent Balance:** Appreciate the adaptability of a Straddler but avoid putting them in the middle of conflicts.

- **Flexible Needs:** Accommodate shifts in a Straddler's priorities. Reassure them of your unconditional love.

Chapter Two

Communication Is Always Key

Healthy, open, and honest communication is essential to any flourishing relationship, be it a romantic partnership or the unique dynamics of a stepchild/stepparent connection. It's a skill that transcends personality types, bridging the gap between individuals whether they lean towards being reserved CDs or outgoing MYs.

In this chapter, let's explore the vital elements of communication that can fortify the bond you share with your stepchild, providing a foundation to lean on in years to come. Furthermore, we'll navigate through the general and distinct traits of each personality type, offering insights on utilizing personality indicators to validate not only your stepchild but also yourself and your needs. This work will set an example for your stepchild, providing them with the skills to articulate themselves in this busy world.

In an era dominated by digital connections and instant gratification, we occasionally overlook the beauty of genuine human interaction. This notion is even more true for your stepchild, as it is likely they have never known life without the internet at their fingertips. The significance of patience, reflection, and being present with our loved ones often eludes all of us. So, take a moment to pause, reflect, and feel as we navigate through this section. By nurturing an atmosphere of open communication and mutual respect, you're not merely constructing relationships and bonds; you're fostering connections that thrive on understanding, compassion, and authentic engagement. Here, we present strategies and guiding principles to effectively express yourself.

Avoid Lecturing

Don't pontificate! Avoiding lectures is an essential part of nurturing a healthy relationship with a stepchild. With their one-sided nature, lectures may inadvertently create a rift in communication and hinder the development of trust with your stepchild. Constructive conversations, on the other hand, are the cornerstone of building a strong bond. They involve engaging in an open dialogue that encourages both parties to participate actively with a give-and-take approach.

Instead of dictating instructions, strive for an open dialogue where your stepchild feels comfortable sharing their thoughts and opinions. You want your stepchild to feel *heard*. This inclusivity not only makes them feel valued but encourages a sense of belonging within the family dynamic. For example, rather than lecturing about curfew times, initiate a conversation where you discuss together what a reasonable curfew might look like considering their responsibilities and your concerns. This collaborative approach fosters mutual respect and understanding, even if you ultimately need to establish a rule they do not care for. They will know that they were heard.

Likewise, open-ended questions play a pivotal role in steering conversations away from lectures. These questions encourage your stepchild to express their thoughts and feelings freely instead of an apathetic yes or no answer. When discussing topics like academic performance or hobbies, ask open-ended questions like, "What subjects in school do you find most interesting, and why?" or "Can you tell me about a project you worked on that you're really proud of?" These questions encourage them to share more about their interests and experiences, allowing for a deeper, more meaningful conversation that goes beyond the surface.

We cannot stress enough how encouraging participation and valuing their input can significantly impact the way your stepchild perceives their role within the family. When discussing family decisions, seek their opinions and incorporate their ideas whenever possible.

For instance, when planning a family outing, ask for their input on the destination or activities they'd like to try. This involvement helps them feel heard and respected, fostering a sense of belonging and collaboration within the family unit. It's not about imposing an agenda but about engaging in discussions that promote mutual understanding and consideration.

Active Listening

Active listening serves as the backbone of effective communication, especially within the complexities of a blended family. It transcends merely hearing words. Active listening is the deciphering of emotions, intentions, and what may be left unsaid.

Engaging in conversations with your stepchild demands a deliberate effort to be wholly present. Through consistent eye contact, nodding in acknowledgment, and offering affirmations like "I understand" or "That makes sense," you convey an active engagement in the dialogue. Reflective listening further solidifies this connection. Paraphrasing their words to ensure understanding—such as affirming, "It sounds like the steps in your dance routine are overwhelming for you. Am I getting that right?"—showcases not just your attentiveness but also your commitment to comprehending their perspective, fostering an environment of trust and transparency.

Demonstrating active listening requires decoding underlying emotions and intentions demonstrated through body language and tone. For instance, when your stepchild discusses an issue at school, observe their mannerisms. Is anything different (or not) in the way they usually sit, talk, or gesticulate? If they seem hesitant or upset while discussing a particular topic, perhaps by holding their breath or scratching at their arms, gently inquire further. Try saying something like, "I notice you seem uneasy talking about this, and I care about you. Is there something more you'd like to share? I am a safe space." Illustrating your genuine interest in understanding their emotional state invites them to delve deeper into their feelings.

Moreover, employing reflective listening techniques encourages a deeper level of engagement. Reiterating their thoughts in your own words not only validates their feelings but ensures clarity and mutual understanding. If your stepchild appears withdrawn or tense during a conversation, consider offering reassurance by expressing, "I sense there might be something on your mind. I'm here whenever you're ready to talk." This acknowledgment of their non-verbal cues demonstrates your sensitivity to their emotions, encouraging them to open up at their own pace.

Neutral Language

Neutral language serves as a powerful tool to maintain harmony and understanding, especially within a blended family context. It involves consciously selecting words and phrases that avoid accusatory or confrontational tones, thereby diffusing potential conflicts.

When discussing sensitive topics such as household responsibilities and chores, reframing your language can significantly alter the course of the conversation and mitigate blowouts. For instance, instead of using phrases that might provoke defensiveness like, "You never help with chores," opt for a neutral and inclusive approach by saying, "It would be great if we could collaborate on household tasks. What can I help you with? What can you help me with?" This subtle shift encourages cooperation rather than assigning blame, fostering an environment conducive to mutual respect and collaboration.

By choosing neutral language, you also redirect the focus from assigning fault to problem-solving. When addressing behavioral concerns or conflicts, framing your thoughts in a non-confrontational manner can lead to more constructive discussions. For instance, rather than saying, "You're always disrespectful," consider a more neutral approach like, "Let's talk about how we can communicate respectfully with each other." This seemingly subtle change in language encourages the development of effective communication skills within the family, also setting an expectation for how your stepchild expects to be treated in the future.

Lastly, neutral language allows for the acknowledgment of differing perspectives without friction. It facilitates open discussions where both parties feel heard and understood. In situations where opinions may clash, neutral language can create a safe space for dialogue. In turn, that makes YOU a safe place for your stepchild.

For example, during discussions about heated topics, instead of imposing directives, try a neutral approach by saying, "Let's find a balance between our different viewpoints on this rule." This technique invites negotiation and compromise, fostering a sense of inclusivity and mutual understanding within the family. Utilizing this approach consistently helps create an environment where conflicts are approached with a focus on resolution rather than blame, contributing to a cohesive blended family dynamic.

Understanding Different Communication Styles

Understanding and accommodating different communication styles is pivotal for fostering meaningful connections. Recognizing that each person, including your stepchild, has a distinct way of expressing themselves lays the groundwork for effective communication. Some children, such as an MY, may feel more comfortable articulating their thoughts directly through conversations, while others, such as CDs, may convey their feelings and emotions more effectively through a retreat into creative outlets like art or activities. Observing and deciphering these cues offers valuable insight into how they prefer to communicate.

Adapting to your stepchild's communication style requires a willingness to meet them on their terms and not just your own. For instance, if your stepchild seems to enjoy drawing or painting, use this as an opportunity to engage in conversations. Ask open-ended questions about their artwork to initiate dialogue, such as, "I noticed you drew a lot of animals in your painting. Can you tell me more about why you chose those animals?" This approach not only encourages them to express themselves but also demonstrates your interest in their unique mode of communication, fostering a stronger bond. They will feel seen and acknowledged.

Moreover, being attentive to non-verbal cues is equally important. Some children may find it challenging to articulate their feelings verbally, but their body language or facial expressions might convey a lot. Paying attention to these non-verbal cues can provide valuable insights into their emotions and thoughts. For instance, if your stepchild appears withdrawn or upset, rather than pressing for verbal explanations, offer them space and support. You might say, "I can see you're feeling upset. If you'd like to talk about it later, I'm here for you." This respectful acknowledgment of their emotions while respecting their need for space communicates your understanding and support, especially for a CD stepchild.

Understanding and adapting to your stepchild's communication style not only enhances your ability to connect but also reinforces the message that you value and respect their individuality. This adaptability paves the way for deeper and more meaningful interactions, nurturing a relationship built on mutual understanding and acceptance. We won't be surprised if they ask a few questions about you too, such as your upbringing or past experiences.

Creating a Safe Space for Expression

Establishing a safe space for your stepchild to express themselves is a foundational pillar in nurturing a healthy relationship. It begins with fostering this concept of openness and acceptance, where they feel secure sharing their thoughts and emotions without fear of criticism or punishment. Start by expressly assuring them that their opinions and feelings are valuable and that they can freely express themselves without judgment. For instance, if your stepchild seems hesitant to discuss school issues, create an inviting environment by saying, "I want you to know that you can talk to me about anything, and I'll listen without judging. Is there anything on your mind that you'd like to share?"

Confidentiality and privacy are essential components of a safe space. Emphasize the importance of keeping their conversations private unless there's a serious concern that requires intervention. You can consider this a balance between being a sounding board for their ideas while also maintaining that you are not the child's parent and that nothing be kept from your spouse. An example scenario might involve your stepchild confiding in you about a friendship problem. You could respond by saying, "I appreciate you telling me about this. I'll keep it between us unless you feel it's necessary for someone else to know, although I hope you know you can share this with your mom/dad. How can I support you through this?" This assurance encourages trust and reassures your stepchild that their confidences are respected and safe while not isolating them from their parents.

Creating an environment where they feel heard and understood is so crucial. Practice active listening without interruptions or judgments when they share their thoughts or experiences. Encourage them to elaborate on their feelings by asking follow-up questions that show genuine interest and concern. Suppose your stepchild expresses frustration about not fitting in with peers at school. In that case, you could respond by asking, "What makes you feel left out? Is there anything specific you wish were different?"

Another aspect of establishing a safe space involves validating their emotions. Acknowledge their feelings and avoid dismissing or minimizing them even if their concerns may seem trivial to you. This validation helps build their emotional intelligence and encourages them to continue sharing their thoughts. For instance, if your stepchild feels upset about a disagreement with a sibling over a toy, you might respond by saying, "It's okay to feel upset. It's tough when we don't agree with someone."

Furthermore, maintaining consistency in your availability and receptiveness is crucial. Ensure that your stepchild knows they can approach you at any time to talk about their concerns or joys. Be present and attentive when they initiate conversations, showing that you value their thoughts and emotions. Do not get lost in your phone and half-listen. Do not continue to do chores in the house while they speak with you. Drop what you are doing! Consistent support and availability create a sense of security, making children more likely to seek guidance or share experiences. This consistency might involve having a designated time for bonding activities, like a weekly movie night or a walk in the park, where they know they can freely express themselves.

Lastly, fostering a safe space involves managing your reactions as well. Be mindful of your responses and avoid overreacting or becoming overly emotional, especially when discussing sensitive topics. Do not make it about you. Your calm and composed demeanor reassures your stepchild that they can openly communicate without fearing negative reactions. Demonstrating patience and empathy in your responses creates an environment where they feel safe to be themselves and openly share their thoughts and feelings.

Communicating Expectations and Support

Establishing clear expectations while providing consistent support is a cornerstone in nurturing a healthy relationship with your stepchild. Start by openly discussing household rules and expectations in the same collaborative manner that has been echoing through this chapter. For example, when setting boundaries regarding screen time, engage your stepchild by saying, "Let's decide on a fair amount of time for screen activities during weekdays together. What do you think is a reasonable limit?" This approach empowers them to participate in the decision-making process and feel more invested in adhering to the agreed-upon rules. Even if you ultimately have to be more conservative on a decision than they would like, they will know that they were supported.

Communicate academic expectations in a supportive manner, emphasizing your willingness to assist and guide them. Discuss the importance of education and encourage them to strive for their personal best, making sure not to deify perfection. Suppose your stepchild is struggling with a particular subject. In that case, offer your help by saying, "I'm here to help if you need extra support with math. Let's work on some practice problems together to make it easier for you." If you are not good at math, offer to find someone who is!

Consistency in communication is crucial in reinforcing expectations. Ensure that the rules are consistently applied to avoid confusion or resentment. Oftentimes, while not always the case, the separation of the child's birth parents can lead to a loss of consistency. Consistency provides a sense of stability and helps your stepchild understand that these expectations are not arbitrary but rooted in care and concern. For instance, if bedtime rules are set, maintain consistency in enforcing them every night, emphasizing the importance of rest for their well-being. Let your consistency create a blanket of safety around them, anchored in dependability.

Supporting your stepchild in meeting these expectations is equally essential. Demonstrate your unwavering encouragement and assistance, making it clear that you're there to help them navigate challenges. For example, if they're responsible for certain household chores, rather than reprimanding them for missed tasks, offer guidance and encouragement. Say, "I know keeping up with chores can be overwhelming. Let's create a checklist or a schedule together to make it more manageable."

Moreover, be mindful of how you express your support. Encourage them by acknowledging their efforts and progress rather than solely focusing on end results. Celebrate the small things! Be their cheerleader, whether it's improvement in academics, successfully completing chores, or displaying good behavior. Acknowledging their efforts motivates them to continue striving for success. For instance, if your stepchild diligently completes their chores without reminders, praise their responsibility by saying, "I noticed how responsible and independent you were in completing your chores without being reminded. That's a great effort!"

Lastly, maintain an open line of communication regarding these expectations. Encourage your stepchild to express any concerns or difficulties they face in meeting these expectations. Listen actively and provide guidance or reassurance where needed. Create an environment where they feel comfortable discussing their challenges or seeking advice without fear of judgment. This open dialogue fosters a sense of trust and mutual understanding, reinforcing the idea that your support is unwavering, regardless of the circumstances.

Model Healthy Communication

If you are following the guidelines in this chapter, you will organically begin to model healthy communication for your stepchild. This model lays the groundwork for developing their own effective communication skills, as you are now one of the most trusted adults in their life. Your interactions, both with them and with others, serve as a blueprint for their understanding of healthy interaction. Demonstrating empathy is key—show genuine concern and understanding when they share their thoughts or concerns. For example, if your stepchild expresses frustration about a disagreement with a friend, respond with empathy by saying, "I can understand why you'd feel upset about that."

Respect in communication is so important and cannot be stressed enough. Exhibit respect toward their opinions and feelings, even if they differ from your own. Encourage them to voice their thoughts without fear of judgment. If discussing conflicting views, model respectful dialogue by saying, "I appreciate your perspective, even though I see things differently. Let's discuss our viewpoints and find some common ground." This approach demonstrates respect for their opinions while encouraging open and respectful discussions.

Patience is a fundamental aspect of healthy communication. Show patience when engaging in conversations, especially during moments of disagreement or frustration. If your stepchild is struggling to articulate their thoughts or feelings, practice patience by allowing them the time they need to express themselves. For instance, if they're hesitant to discuss a sensitive issue, assure them that you're patient and willing to listen whenever they're ready.

Modeling conflict resolution is crucial in shaping their approach to handling disagreements. Show them how conflicts can be resolved through calm discussions and compromise rather than arguments or hostility. For instance, if there's a disagreement over a family decision, demonstrate compromise by saying, "Let's find a solution that works for both of us. What suggestions do you have, and how can we meet halfway?"

Moreover, acknowledge and rectify mistakes when they occur. We are all only human. Model accountability by admitting when you've made an error or handled a situation poorly. Showing humility in acknowledging your mistakes demonstrates to your stepchild that it's okay to be imperfect and that learning from mistakes is an essential part of healthy communication. This openness cultivates an environment where they feel comfortable admitting their errors and learning from them. No one is perfect.

Embracing Emotional Expression

Encouraging emotional expression in your stepchild cultivates a safe and supportive environment for them to freely express their feelings. Start by demonstrating that both positive and negative emotions are accepted and valued. If your stepchild expresses excitement about a personal achievement, celebrate their success wholeheartedly. Acknowledge their joy by saying, "I'm so proud of your accomplishment! It's wonderful to see your hard work pay off." Similarly, when they convey feelings of disappointment or sadness, validate their emotions by expressing understanding and empathy. For instance, if they're upset about not making a sports team, reassure them by saying, "I understand you're feeling disappointed. It's okay to feel that way, and I'm here for you always."

Creating an open dialogue about emotions involves normalizing the expression of feelings. Encourage discussions about emotions by initiating conversations that explore various emotional experiences. For example, during a movie or book discussion, ask them about the characters' emotions and how they relate to similar feelings they might have experienced. This approach allows them to reflect on their emotions in a comfortable setting, fostering emotional awareness and understanding. It also allows them to process what they are learning in this reflection and active engagement with you.

Furthermore, teaching them about emotional regulation and healthy coping strategies is valuable. Help them recognize different emotions and provide guidance on ways to manage and express these feelings. If they're feeling overwhelmed or upset, suggest relaxation techniques like deep breathing or journaling. By offering practical tools to manage complex emotions, you equip them with skills to take with them far into adulthood and beyond.

Additionally, lead by example in healthily managing your own emotions. When faced with stressful situations, demonstrate how to handle emotions calmly and constructively. For instance, if you encounter a frustrating situation, model coping mechanisms by saying, "I'm feeling frustrated right now, but I'm going to take a few deep breaths to calm down before responding." This demonstration of emotional regulation underscores the importance of managing emotions in a positive way. Supporting your stepchild in expressing emotions also involves providing a non-judgmental space for discussions. When they express challenging emotions like anger or fear, avoid dismissing or trivializing their feelings. Instead, listen attentively, validate their emotions, and offer guidance on how to navigate these feelings constructively.

Humanize Yourself

Humanizing yourself to your stepchild involves sharing relatable experiences that showcase your vulnerability and humanity. Once upon a time, you were a little kid full of wonder or an angsty teen looking to fit in. When appropriate, share those personal stories from your past that reflect challenges or moments of growth, or perhaps just something fun. For instance, you might share a story about a time when you felt nervous before a big event or struggled with a difficult decision. This transparency creates a relatable connection. They will know in concrete ways that you've faced challenges too, making it easier for your stepchild to relate to you and confide in you without fear of judgment.

Moreover, sharing your own experiences allows your stepchild to see you as more than just an authority figure or the person who is romantically attached to their parent. You are a trusted family member with your own vulnerabilities, thoughts, and feelings. Demonstrating vulnerability in appropriate situations can deepen your bond with your stepchild. It can be as simple as acknowledging when you make a mistake or apologizing if you've misunderstood their feelings. This vulnerability communicates humility and sincerity, showing them that it's okay to make mistakes and that learning from them is important. For example, if you misunderstand their feelings about a particular situation, admit your mistake by saying, "I'm sorry, I misunderstood how you were feeling. Can you help me understand better?"

Furthermore, engaging in activities together where you're both learning or trying something new can also humanize you in their eyes and level the playing field. Whether it's learning a new skill, trying a new hobby, or even just playing a new board game together, being open to learning alongside them emphasizes that you're not only a guide but also someone who's constantly growing and evolving. This shared experience creates a sense of camaraderie and mutual respect, reinforcing the idea that learning and adapting are ongoing processes for everyone. You want them to be a lifelong learner, too.

The key takeaway in this section is to be sure to create a balance between being an authority figure and a relatable mentor. While it's important to share personal stories, it's equally essential to maintain boundaries and appropriate levels of authority when needed. This balance establishes a healthy dynamic where they feel supported and understood while respecting your guidance. Showing vulnerability doesn't diminish your role as a responsible adult; rather, it strengthens the bond by fostering mutual trust and understanding.

By incorporating these communication strategies into your relationship with your stepchild, you'll create a foundation of understanding, trust, and respect. Effective communication lays the groundwork for a healthy and loving relationship, nurturing a bond that only grows stronger over time.

Chapter Three
Emotional Closeness

Welcome to a chapter dedicated solely to fostering emotional closeness with your stepchild. In this section, we'll explore several best practices designed to strengthen your bond and create a space where understanding and connection flourish. From engaging in meaningful conversations and allowing them to guide the way to respecting their thoughts and expressions, we'll navigate the terrain of building a relationship founded on trust and mutual respect. By participating in shared activities, acknowledging their potential emotional struggles, and being receptive to their needs, you'll be laying the groundwork for a deeper, more meaningful connection. Remember, it's not just about avoiding criticism; it's about recognizing and praising their strengths while showering them with the affection that forms the genuine and loving relationship you seek to cultivate through this work.

Talk to Them

Initiating conversations serves as a gateway to building emotional intimacy with your stepchild. Engage in discussions about their passions, interests, or mundane daily experiences to create a comfortable space for open dialogue regardless of the topic. If they're passionate about astronomy, ask about their favorite constellations or space discoveries, allowing them to share their knowledge and passions with you. In turn, tell them that you like hearing what they have to say about astronomy, and ask thoughtful questions. This approach not only showcases your interest but also encourages them to express themselves freely, fostering a sense of connection.

Ask open-ended questions that encourage them to reflect on their experiences or share their thoughts on broader topics. For instance, discuss current events or societal issues in an age-appropriate manner. Asking questions like, "What do you think about kindness in our community? How can we contribute to making it better?" initiates discussions that stimulate critical thinking and reflection, fostering deeper connections and demonstrating the value you place on their opinions.

Discussing their school life or daily activities may also help bridge the communication gap. This conversation might uncover aspects of their life that they're eager to share but haven't had the opportunity to discuss. For example, inquiring about a school project they're excited about allows them to delve into their interests and achievements and emphasizes your willingness to listen and engage in their experiences. You can ask about their day, interesting events at school, or their favorite subjects, although we know at times this can be challenging with adolescent and teenage stepchildren. Conversations do not need to always be lengthy or involved to be meaningful or establish this bond. Pick up on their cues and...

Let Them Take the Lead

Encouraging your stepchild to take the lead in conversations or activities is a great way to empower them and nurture their sense of autonomy. When they express interest in a particular topic, hobby, or outing, allow them to spearhead the planning or decision-making process, showcasing your respect for their preferences and opinions. For example, if they express a keen interest in hiking, let them take charge by researching trails, planning the route, or even leading the hike. This approach not only validates their choices but also instills confidence in their decision-making abilities, and it can be scaffolded to meet any age.

Furthermore, giving them the freedom to steer conversations fosters an environment where their thoughts and feelings are heard and valued. Suppose they show enthusiasm for discussing a topic or sharing a story. In that case, encourage them to lead the conversation by actively listening and providing them with the space to express themselves. This initiative demonstrates your trust in their ability to contribute meaningfully to the conversation, reinforcing their sense of importance within the family dynamic.

Moreover, embracing their leadership in certain situations encourages their personal growth and independence. Suppose they're an MY, very eager to take on responsibilities or tasks. In that case, allowing them to lead the way in completing those tasks, whether it's organizing a family game night or managing a small household project, reinforces their confidence and capabilities. This empowerment promotes a sense of accomplishment and reinforces the notion that their contributions are integral to the family's dynamics. If they are more reserved and a CD, gently encouraging them to adopt responsibilities or tasks can help prepare them for the real world.

Respect Their Minds

Respecting your stepchild's thoughts is a key step that must be taken. Encouraging them to express their viewpoints even when they differ from your own creates an environment of openness and mutual respect. Suppose they hold a different perspective on a family decision or express thoughts contrary to your own. In that scenario, validate their opinions by expressing appreciation for their viewpoint. For instance, if they disagree with a household rule, acknowledge their perspective by saying, "I see where you're coming from. It's important to consider everyone's thoughts. Let's talk about how we can find a solution that works for all of us."

As we have been discussing, fostering an atmosphere where diverse opinions are welcomed promotes critical thinking and confidence in expressing thoughts. Encourage debates or discussions on topics where their input is valued but without condescending or negativity. For instance, if discussing a current event or a family decision, encourage them to share their thoughts and actively engage in the discussion. Acknowledging their contributions and perspectives validates their sense of importance within the family dynamic, fostering a sense of trust and openness.

Additionally, modeling respect for differing opinions is essential. Demonstrate acceptance and openness when your stepchild expresses thoughts that contrast with yours. If they challenge your views, continue to respond with patience and understanding. For example, if they express an opinion on a movie or book that contradicts your own, engage in a discussion that acknowledges their perspective without dismissing it. This approach encourages them to voice their opinions confidently without fear of judgment. You are able to be honest and forthcoming, but patient and kind.

Furthermore, teaching them about respectful communication in expressing differing opinions is crucial. Encourage them to express their thoughts assertively and respectfully, understanding that disagreements can be healthy when communicated with respect. Tone and word choice are essential here. Guide them in articulating their viewpoints in a way that contributes to constructive discussions rather than conflicts. This guidance helps them navigate disagreements in a respectful manner, fostering an environment where differing opinions are valued and understood.

Respect Their Expression

Acknowledging and accepting your stepchild's emotions, irrespective of whether they're positive or negative, creates an environment where they feel understood and supported. Suppose they're distressed about a disagreement with a friend. They may be quiet, or they could be in a well of tears. In either case, refrain from minimizing their feelings and instead validate their emotions. Acknowledge their distress by saying, "It's tough to have conflicts with friends. I'm here to listen if you'd like to talk about it," indicating your willingness to support them without imposing your version of a solution.

Furthermore, showing empathy and understanding during moments of emotional expression serves to reinforce the trust you are working so hard to establish. If your stepchild is experiencing frustration or sadness, offer a compassionate response rather than immediately trying to resolve the issue, as hard as that may be. Express understanding by saying, "I can see this is upsetting for you. Take your time. I'm here whenever you're ready to talk." This allows them to process emotions at their own pace. This empathetic approach communicates that their feelings are valid and respected, fostering a sense of security in expressing their emotions openly.

Moreover, refrain from judging or criticizing their feelings even if they differ from your own perceptions. If they express emotions that you might not fully understand or agree with, avoid dismissing their feelings. Instead, validate their experiences by saying, "I may not completely understand, but your feelings are important to me. How can I support you through this?" This approach conveys acceptance and support, reassuring them that it's okay to express themselves without fear of judgment.

Additionally, provide reassurance that expressing emotions is healthy and normal. Encourage them to express themselves without bottling up their feelings. Creating an open dialogue about emotions emphasizes that it's okay to share feelings and seek support when needed. Encourage them by saying, "It's okay to feel upset or frustrated. It's important to talk about how we feel. I'm here whenever you need to talk or share what's on your mind," fosters an environment where emotional expression is valued and embraced.

Have Meaningful Interactions

Having meaningful interactions with your stepchild goes beyond casual conversations and delves into topics that hold significance to them. Exploring subjects that resonate deeply, such as their aspirations, anxieties, or worries, establishes a space for emotional connection. For example, initiate a discussion about their ambitions or apprehensions regarding their future. Asking questions like, "What are your dreams for the future? Are there any concerns you have about the changes ahead?" invites them to open up about their thoughts and feelings, creating an environment where they feel heard and valued.

Moreover, these meaningful exchanges provide opportunities for you to organically offer guidance and support. Suppose your stepchild expresses concerns about transitioning to a new school. In that case, engage in a conversation that acknowledges their worries and offers reassurance that you and your spouse will always be there. Share your own experiences of navigating changes or offer advice on adapting to new environments. This supportive approach demonstrates your understanding and willingness to help them navigate through their concerns.

Additionally, discussing deeper topics showcases your genuine interest in their well-being and reinforces the notion that their thoughts and feelings matter. Engage in conversations that revolve around their passions, values, or perspectives on societal issues. For instance, discussing their opinions on kindness, empathy, or community involvement fosters thought-provoking discussions that encourage critical thinking and empathy. These conversations offer opportunities to understand their values and beliefs while allowing them to express their thoughts freely.

Furthermore, demonstrating empathy during these meaningful interactions is crucial. Show empathy by actively listening, validating their emotions, and offering understanding. If they share worries or concerns, respond by acknowledging their feelings and offering comfort. Saying, "We all have concerns about new experiences. I'm here to support you and help in any way I can," reassures them that you're a supportive figure they can rely on during challenging times. This empathetic approach nurtures a deeper bond built on trust and understanding.

Engage in Activities Together

Engaging in activities alongside your stepchild is a powerful way to strengthen your bond and create cherished memories. Shared experiences like cooking a meal together, engaging in a sport, or working on a project offer valuable opportunities for connection and emotional closeness. Suppose you embark on a DIY project together. Not only does it facilitate collaboration and problem-solving, but it creates a platform for meaningful conversation and bonding. As you work side by side assembling furniture or crafting something, it opens avenues for relaxed and genuine conversations, fostering a deeper connection. Whether it is a work of art or a Pinterest fail, the important thing is that you do it together!

Furthermore, these shared activities provide a natural setting for communication and understanding that isn't forced. For instance, participating in a cooking session naturally allows for shared responsibilities, communication, and teamwork. Whether it's preparing a favorite dish or trying out a new recipe, this collaborative effort not only strengthens your relationship but also allows for light-hearted conversation, creating moments that deepen your emotional connection.

Moreover, engaging in physical activities or sports together encourages a sense of camaraderie and shared accomplishment. Whether it's shooting hoops, going for a hike, or playing a board game, these activities promote teamwork, laughter, and bonding. Suppose you engage in a sport together like shooting hoops in the backyard. This presents an opportunity to enjoy each other's company, share lighthearted moments, and perhaps even engage in friendly competition, strengthening the emotional connection through shared enjoyment. Remember, it feels good to get the body moving along with the mind.

Understand They May Be Hurting

Acknowledging that your stepchild might be grappling with emotional challenges from past experiences is a key turning point in going from someone Mom or Dad is involved with to a bona fide family member. They could be processing emotions tied to family dynamics or previous relationships in or outside the family. Being attuned to signs of distress or withdrawal, such as sudden mood changes or social isolation, allows you to offer support without imposing. For instance, if you notice changes in their behavior, like retreating to their room more frequently, offer them space while also expressing your availability whenever they're ready to talk. This approach conveys your support while respecting their need for privacy.

Moreover, creating a safe and non-judgmental space for them to share their emotions is crucial. It's essential to reassure them that it's okay not to share everything but that you're there whenever they're ready. Consider initiating conversations that gently probe their emotions without pressure. For instance, saying, "I've noticed you've seemed a bit quieter lately. If there's anything on your mind, I'm here to listen," provides an opening for them to express themselves without feeling obligated.

Additionally, offering avenues for emotional expression beyond verbal communication can be beneficial. Introducing activities like journaling, art, or music provides alternative outlets for them to process their emotions. If your stepchild enjoys drawing or painting, encourage them to express their feelings through art, or buy them a journal. This creative expression allows them to externalize their emotions without the pressure of verbalizing them, promoting emotional healing and understanding. They will know that you thought of them.

Furthermore, seeking professional support or counseling might be beneficial if your stepchild is grappling with deeper emotional distress. If you notice persistent signs of distress or behavioral changes that impact their well-being, consider discussing the option of professional guidance in consultation with your spouse. Express your support and willingness to help them navigate their emotions by saying, "I've noticed you might be going through a tough time. Would you like to talk to someone who can help you understand your feelings better?" This proactive approach shows your commitment to their emotional well-being and reinforces your support during challenging times while respecting the relationship between them and their parent.

Let Them Tell You What They Need

Oftentimes, adults impose their own needs or concepts of what a child may want. Encouraging your stepchild to vocalize their needs and desires strengthens the bond between you. This approach allows the stepchild to be their own person and define their terms. Suppose they express a desire for more one-on-one time with their parent. In that case, acknowledging and respecting their requests is crucial. For instance, if they ask for dedicated time to engage in an activity just with your spouse, try to carve out that space, demonstrating your willingness to prioritize their needs and realize it is not always about you.

Likewise, showing attentiveness to their needs involves creating an environment where they feel comfortable expressing themselves without hesitation. Suppose your stepchild communicates a need for privacy or space. In that case, respecting their boundaries without prying or making them feel obligated to divulge further ensures they feel respected and understood. For example, if they request time alone in their room, honor their request while expressing your availability if they wish to talk or spend time together later.

Additionally, fostering an open dialogue about their preferences and requirements encourages a healthy exchange of thoughts and feelings. Actively engage in discussions about what makes them comfortable or changes they wish to see within the home or beyond. For instance, initiating a conversation about their preferred study space or how they enjoy spending their free time invites them to express their preferences and needs comfortably. This engagement demonstrates your respect for their autonomy and promotes an environment where their opinions are valued.

Furthermore, demonstrating flexibility and willingness to accommodate their needs within reason reinforces their sense of importance and consideration. If they express a desire for certain activities or adjustments within the household routine, discuss and explore possible ways to accommodate their requests. For example, if they express a preference for a particular meal or suggest a change in a family tradition, consider incorporating their input whenever feasible. You are a new family now. This collaborative approach communicates that their voice matters and that you're open to considering their needs and preferences.

Praise Them

Acknowledging and praising your stepchild's efforts and achievements is instrumental in fostering their self-esteem and reinforcing positive behavior. Celebrating accomplishments, regardless of their magnitude, communicates your appreciation and support. For example, recognizing their diligence in completing a school project or highlighting their acts of kindness towards a sibling reinforces these positive traits. When you praise them for specific actions or behaviors, it encourages repetition and reinforces the importance of those behaviors within the family dynamic.

Moreover, praising their efforts rather than focusing solely on outcomes instills a sense of resilience and determination. Acknowledge the process and dedication they invest in their endeavors, emphasizing the value of hard work and perseverance. For instance, if they put effort into improving a skill, commend their dedication and progress rather than solely focusing on the final result. This approach reinforces a growth mindset, encouraging them to keep striving for improvement.

Additionally, offering praise for their unique strengths and qualities fosters a sense of individuality and self-worth. Highlighting their attributes or talents, such as creativity, kindness, or empathy, reinforces these positive aspects of their personality. For example, acknowledging their creativity in solving a problem or appreciating their empathetic nature towards a friend's feelings validates and encourages these traits.

Furthermore, integrating praise into everyday interactions creates a culture of positivity and encouragement within the family. Expressing gratitude for their contributions to household tasks or acknowledging their positive attitude during challenging times reinforces a supportive environment. If they take the initiative to help with chores without being asked, acknowledging their contribution by saying, "I noticed how helpful you've been with tidying up. Your effort really makes a difference around here," reinforces their sense of responsibility and contribution to the family.

Lastly, it is extremely helpful to also praise your stepchild around other people so they can witness firsthand how you perceive them and all they've achieved, no matter how small. For example, if your stepchild works hard to prepare a dinner for the family, convey your feelings of pride by saying to your spouse, "Did you taste how good the bolognese is tonight? [Child's name] makes the best food." There is no doubt they will be smiling from ear to ear when they hear you say this. This consistent acknowledgment fosters a sense of belonging and appreciation.

Show Them Affection

Expressing affection towards your stepchild is a fundamental way to reinforce emotional bonds and create a supportive atmosphere within the family. Demonstrating love and appreciation through gestures, verbal affirmations, and appropriate physical displays of affection establishes a sense of security and belonging. For instance, offering hugs or verbal expressions of affection such as saying "I love you" or "I'm proud of you" communicates your care and reinforces the emotional connection between you and your stepchild.

Moreover, incorporating small gestures of affection into daily interactions reinforces feelings of closeness and connection. Simple acts like leaving encouraging notes in their lunchbox, complimenting their efforts, or initiating a warm embrace after a long day show that you value and cherish their presence in your life. For instance, leaving a note expressing appreciation for their helpfulness or resilience in overcoming challenges communicates your recognition and affection.

Additionally, understanding and respecting their preferences regarding affectionate gestures is essential. Some individuals prefer verbal affirmations while others might feel more comfortable with physical displays of affection. What is your stepchild's love language? Being mindful of their comfort levels and preferences ensures that your gestures of affection are received positively. For example, respecting their boundaries by asking if they're comfortable with a hug or a high-five before initiating physical contact reinforces their sense of agency and respect within the relationship.

Furthermore, consistency in displaying affection creates a sense of emotional security and stability. Regularly expressing love and appreciation, regardless of the circumstances, reinforces the understanding that your affection is constant and unconditional. Whether it's through a daily "good morning" hug or an evening affirmation, this consistent display of affection fosters a sense of trust and reassurance, strengthening the emotional bond between you and your stepchild.

Chapter Four

Navigating Social Needs

Now that we've explored emotional closeness, let's begin to delve into the intricacies of your stepchild's social needs. In the pages ahead, we'll explore the art of understanding and respecting their social needs, fostering independence, and creating a supportive space where they can navigate the complex emotions that may arise. We'll discuss the importance of allowing space and privacy, recognizing potential feelings of being torn, and offering unyielding support. So, let's continue this journey as we discover how persistence in maintaining an active role in your stepchild's life will weave a fabric of belonging and unity within your new family.

Understand and Respect Their Social Needs

Understanding and respecting your stepchild's interpersonal needs involves acknowledging and honoring their preferences for social interactions or solitude in keeping with our work on personality types. For example, if your stepchild is primarily an MY, encourage and support their interactions with friends. You can facilitate these interactions by arranging outings or gatherings to encourage them to connect and build relationships. On the other hand, if they tend to be more of a CD, respect their need for personal space and quiet time. Providing an environment that allows them to recharge and pursue their interests independently validates their needs and promotes a sense of autonomy and comfort within the family setting. If you find yourself with a Straddler stepchild, learn to balance the approach based on where they are at that point in time.

Observing and responding to their social inclinations plays a significant role in creating a supportive atmosphere aligned with their preferences. Suppose your stepchild expresses a desire to spend more time with friends. In that case, actively facilitating these opportunities showcases your understanding and support for their social needs. Similarly, if they seek moments of solitude, ensuring they have a designated space where they can unwind and enjoy their own company communicates respect for their boundaries and fosters a sense of security and belonging. It is all about the needs of the child.

Recognizing and adjusting to their social inclinations can also involve engaging in open conversations about their preferences. If you are not sure how they feel about a particular scenario, simply ask them. Encouraging them to express their desires and needs regarding social interactions provides a platform for mutual understanding. Whether it's organizing social outings or creating designated quiet spaces within the home, this dialogue allows you to tailor the family environment to better accommodate their preferences.

Furthermore, being flexible and adaptable to their changing social needs over time is crucial. Adolescents, for instance, might experience shifts in their social preferences as they navigate different phases of growth and development, especially as they move into their teenage years. Staying attuned to these changes and adjusting your approach accordingly demonstrates your commitment to understanding and respecting their evolving social needs, ultimately strengthening your relationship. With all of the associated hormonal changes, puberty and beyond are challenging times not just physically but socially. It is important to heed these changes and proceed with grace.

Engage in Activities With Them

Engaging in activities alongside your stepchild is a powerful means of building mutual trust. Participating in activities that align with their interests demonstrates your genuine interest in their world. Similarly, actively participating in their preferred activities, such as sports or hobbies, strengthens the relationship through shared experiences and quality time spent together. If they're enthusiastic about a particular sport, joining them for a game or practice showcases your support and encouragement. It offers a platform for mutual enjoyment and can even provide opportunities for coaching or guidance, further reinforcing the bond by showing your involvement and interest in their passions. It is important to remember you do not need to be good at these activities; it is about participation.

Moreover, the shared experiences gained from these activities create lasting memories that contribute to the foundation of a strong relationship. For instance, embarking on a hiking trip, attending a concert, or exploring a new hobby together fosters shared moments that become cherished memories. These shared experiences not only deepen your emotional connection but also serve as a means of understanding each other's strengths, preferences, and perspectives.

Furthermore, engaging in activities also offers a platform for fostering open communication and understanding. During these shared moments, casual conversations flow more naturally, enabling you to delve into their thoughts, feelings, and aspirations. For instance, while engaged in a cooking session together, conversations about their school, friends, or future goals can unfold organically. This natural dialogue strengthens the bond by offering insights into their world and providing opportunities to offer guidance or support when needed.

Co-parent and Help Set Boundaries

Collaborating effectively with your spouse in co-parenting is crucial for the well-being and stability of your stepchild as well as the other parent with whom your spouse shares this child. Establishing consistency in rules, expectations, and discipline strategies between both households is pivotal. For instance, suppose bedtime rules or screen time limitations differ between households. In that case, aligning on these aspects as much as possible ensures a unified approach, minimizing confusion or conflict for your stepchild. The child will know what to expect and find safety in familiar routine even when moving between different homes.

Aligning discipline strategies is equally important in co-parenting and perhaps more challenging, as each person approaches this topic with their own perspective. Consistency in how behavioral issues are addressed helps your stepchild understand the boundaries and expectations across both households. For example, if one household has specific consequences for certain behaviors, ensuring these consequences are acknowledged and consistent in both homes aids in reinforcing these boundaries and their importance.

Establishing common ground regarding rules and expectations requires open and respectful communication between co-parents, which also may be difficult. This might involve discussing and negotiating different parenting styles or approaches to discipline. Finding a middle ground that prioritizes the child's best interests while respecting each parent's values and perspectives lays a stable foundation for the child's growth and development. Remember in these discussions that it is the child at the heart of them, not the complexities of your spouse's former relationship with the co-parent.

Furthermore, maintaining communication and flexibility in co-parenting is essential, especially in evolving situations or when dealing with changing circumstances. For instance, if a significant event occurs in either household that might impact the established rules or routines, having open discussions and being willing to adapt and accommodate these changes fosters a supportive environment for the child. Being adaptable and solution-oriented demonstrates a united front between households, reassuring your stepchild of the collaborative effort invested in their well-being and upbringing.

Encourage Them to Spend Time With Friends

Encouraging your stepchild to socialize with friends is a vital part of their development. Providing opportunities for them to engage in social activities outside the family fosters crucial skills and emotional growth. For instance, if your stepchild expresses an interest in participating in community events or joining a club, supporting and facilitating their involvement in such activities demonstrates your encouragement for their social interactions beyond home and school. Your local library, playground, or YMCA can be a great and inexpensive resource for these types of interactions if they do not already have a network they can draw from.

Facilitating time with friends helps your stepchild form bonds and cultivate essential social skills to be a successful adult. Encouraging outings, whether it's inviting friends over for a movie night or supporting their attendance at social gatherings, allows them to learn about cooperation, empathy, and communication in various social settings. For instance, if they're interested in a hobby or sport, encouraging them to join related groups or attend related events can help foster friendships centered around shared interests.

Encouraging and fostering these interactions strengthens their sense of belonging and acceptance among peers. Supporting their social engagements demonstrates your investment in their social development. It could be as simple as arranging playdates for younger children or facilitating transportation for older kids to social events. These actions convey your support and reinforce the importance of cultivating friendships and maintaining healthy social connections.

As we all know, having a circle of friends provides emotional support and companionship for people of any age and any personality type, especially during challenging times. Encouraging them to spend time with friends during transitions or difficult situations allows them to lean on their support network, promoting resilience and emotional strength. Additionally, these friendships can serve as a platform for sharing experiences and feelings, contributing positively to their overall happiness and mental health.

Socialize as a Family Unit

Socializing as a family is instrumental in nurturing a sense of unity. Regular family game nights, outings, or shared vacations offer opportunities for connection and creating cherished memories. For instance, organizing a weekly movie night where everyone gets to pick a movie promotes inclusivity and involvement. This shared experience not only brings joy but also reinforces the idea of togetherness, making everyone feel heard and valued within the family. They will look back fondly on these nights in years to come and will take cues from these experiences when forging their own family.

Family outings or visits to community events offer more opportunities for shared experiences. Attending local fairs, volunteering together, or exploring new places as a family allows for bonding over new discoveries and shared interests. For instance, visiting museums and parks or participating in charity events can be educational and entertaining, fostering mutual respect and a sense of camaraderie among family members.

Moreover, these shared experiences create lasting memories that contribute to the family's collective identity. Whether it's an annual tradition or trying out new activities together, these moments become treasured memories that strengthen the familial bond. For instance, setting aside time for a regular family hike or a themed dinner night builds anticipation and excitement, creating a sense of unity and tradition within the family. These shared experiences become part of the family narrative, reinforcing the idea of being part of a loving and supportive family unit.

Support and Praise Independence

Supporting and praising your stepchild's strides toward independence is crucial in fostering their growth and self-assurance. Acknowledging their initiatives and efforts towards self-reliance reinforces their sense of capability and autonomy. For instance, praising their responsible behavior, such as completing chores without reminders or managing their school responsibilities effectively, affirms their competence and encourages them to take ownership of their actions. Help equip them to take charge of their future with a guiding hand!

Encouraging their independence doesn't just entail praising their achievements; you can also provide opportunities for them to make decisions and take on responsibilities. Allowing them to make age-appropriate choices or giving them tasks that contribute to the household empowers them to develop critical decision-making skills and a sense of accountability. For instance, involving them in planning a family outing or assigning them tasks that contribute to family events fosters their sense of responsibility and capability. Likewise, empowering the child when appropriate to make phone calls to agencies to ask questions and advocate for themselves achieves this as well. For example, if a prospective college student has a question about financial aid, encourage them to pick up the phone and call!

Moreover, offering guidance and support while they navigate their independent endeavors communicates your availability and willingness to assist when needed. For instance, if they're working on a personal project, being available to provide advice or resources demonstrates your support without overshadowing their autonomy. This approach fosters an environment where they feel empowered to explore their interests and capabilities while knowing they have a reliable support system.

Allow Them Space and Privacy

Respecting your stepchild's need for space and privacy is essential in building trust and showing respect for their independence. Providing them with a designated private area such as their own room establishes a sense of ownership and sanctuary within the home. For instance, ensuring they have a space where they can retreat, unwind, and express themselves freely reinforces their sense of belonging and independence. Make an effort to help them decorate and adorn that space with their favorite pictures and colors. If they must share a room, make sure to create their own section with their personalization in mind. Everyone needs a safe place to land.

Respecting boundaries goes beyond physical space; it extends to their personal matters and internal thoughts. Avoiding prying into their personal affairs or forcing them to share information they're not comfortable with demonstrates your acknowledgment of them. For instance, refraining from probing about their feelings or experiences unless they choose to share encourages open communication based on trust rather than coercion.

Knocking and seeking permission to enter before entering their private space communicates respect for their boundaries. This simple gesture demonstrates your acknowledgment of their need for privacy and reinforces the idea that their space is respected and protected. For example, consistently practicing the habit of knocking and waiting for acknowledgment before entering their room fosters a sense of trust and mutual respect within the household. By modeling this behavior, they will learn to extend this courtesy to you.

Moreover, giving them time allows for self-reflection and personal growth will prepare them to be a successful adult. These skills help to rid the mind of the clutter and overstimulation that day-to-day life bombards us with. Respecting their need for occasional isolation communicates understanding and support for their emotional well-being. For instance, understanding and allowing them quiet time after a stressful day or a social event can be crucial in recharging their energy and promoting mental clarity and stability. This acknowledgment and facilitation of their need for solitude promotes a healthy balance between social engagement and personal introspection.

Understand They May Feel Torn

Understanding and acknowledging your stepchild's emotional conflicts between households is vital in providing the support they need during challenging times. Transitioning between households can evoke feelings of confusion or distress. Being empathetic and offering support during these transitions can alleviate their emotional burden. For instance, if they seem hesitant or emotional before leaving for the other parent's house, being attentive and acknowledging their feelings without judgment creates a safe space for them to express their emotions. We all get bogged down by transitions. Hold space in your heart for your stepchild in these moments.

Acknowledging their feelings and experiences without criticism or blame reinforces your role as a supportive figure. It's essential to avoid dismissing or downplaying their emotions, as this might discourage them from expressing themselves openly in the future. For example, if they express sadness or frustration about shifting between homes, validating their feelings by saying, "It's okay to feel this way, and I'm here to support you," continues to emphasize your understanding and willingness to be a source of comfort.

Providing a listening ear during these transitions can be immensely beneficial. Offering them the opportunity to share their thoughts, worries, or anxieties about moving between households fosters open communication and trust. For instance, asking open-ended questions like, "How are you feeling about the transition this week?" shows your interest in their emotions and reinforces that their feelings are acknowledged and valued.

Additionally, being adaptable and flexible during these transitions can help ease the emotional tension. Accommodating their emotional needs by allowing some flexibility in schedules or activities during these times demonstrates your understanding and empathy. For instance, if they need additional time to adjust after arriving at a new household, allowing a brief period for them to settle before engaging in planned activities can be beneficial in easing their transition. This flexible approach reinforces your support and understanding of their emotional struggles during these challenging moments. Remind them that it is okay to experience contradictory emotions at the same time and that it is possible to be both happy and sad, confused and overjoyed, or excited and scared.

Offer Support

Consistent support, irrespective of the situation, is foundational in demonstrating your unwavering commitment to your stepchild's well-being. This support can manifest in various forms from assisting with homework to providing emotional guidance during challenging moments. For instance, offering help with school assignments or projects demonstrates your willingness to contribute to their academic success while fostering a sense of reliability and dependability.

Emotional support during tough times is equally essential. Being present and available when they need someone to talk to establishes a sense of trust and security. For example, if they're dealing with friendship issues or facing difficulties at school, being a compassionate listener and offering guidance without judgment helps them navigate these challenges. Your consistent availability during these moments reinforces that they can rely on you for support and guidance.

Consistency in offering support also involves actively participating in their activities and interests. Engaging in activities they enjoy, such as attending their sports games or artistic performances, shows your interest and encouragement in their passions. These sentiments have echoed through this chapter and ring especially true in this instance. Moreover, this active involvement not only strengthens your bond but also communicates your support and pride in their endeavors.

Moreover, being proactive in anticipating their needs and concerns contributes significantly to their sense of security. For instance, if they have an important exam approaching or a significant event happening, offering encouragement, assistance, or even a simple gesture like preparing their favorite meal can alleviate stress and reinforce your dedication to their well-being. This proactive approach demonstrates your commitment to being a reliable and supportive figure in their life, fostering a stronger bond built on trust and care.

Be Persistent in Maintaining an Active Role

Being persistent and consistently involved in your stepchild's life is key to reinforcing your commitment and dedication to their well-being. Showing genuine interest and actively participating in their life events, whether big or small, establishes a sense of reliability and care. For instance, attending their school events, such as parent-teacher conferences or school performances, demonstrates your genuine interest in their academic progress and overall development.

Consistency in your presence and involvement, irrespective of the situation, solidifies your role as a dependable figure in their life. For example, being available to celebrate their achievements, console them during setbacks, or simply engage in everyday conversations reinforces that you're there for them in every aspect of their life. This unwavering support creates a sense of security and trust in your relationship.

Maintaining an active role involves being proactive in understanding their needs and interests. Actively participating in activities they enjoy or engaging in hobbies together strengthens your bond. For instance, if they show an interest in a particular hobby or sport, dedicating time to learn about it or engage with them in that activity not only fosters shared experiences but also communicates your genuine interest in their passions.

Persistently maintaining an active role involves adapting to their evolving needs and interests. Being open to changes and accommodating their preferences reinforces your willingness to be a supportive presence in their life. For instance, as they grow older, their interests, priorities, and challenges may change. Being flexible and adaptive in your approach demonstrates your commitment to being a constant and supportive figure throughout their journey.

Each of these aspects contributes to fostering a strong and trusting relationship with your stepchild, creating a supportive and nurturing environment within the family.

Chapter Five

Balance a Happy Family Dynamic

What exactly is a family dynamic? And how can we best ensure that we develop strong, long-lasting relationships with our family members? Well, a strong family bond is built upon an enduring foundation of trust, communication, mutual respect, and a sense of belonging. It transcends conventional structures and encompasses diverse family dynamics, including scenarios involving stepchildren and stepparents, as we have explored in this book. These relationships thrive on various elements that contribute to their strength and resilience, which we will continue to discover in this chapter.

Trust forms the cornerstone of a robust family relationship. It's all about creating an environment where every member feels secure, valued, and confident in each other's reliability. In non-traditional family settings like those involving stepchildren and stepparents, trust evolves gradually over time and cannot be rushed. It involves showing up each day for your stepchild. Additionally, open, honest communication plays a pivotal role in establishing trust. You must take the initiative to listen, understand, and validate your stepchild's feelings and experiences to foster trust.

Communication is another vital component, which we well know. In this context, strong family relationships are continually nurtured through effective and compassionate communication. In non-traditional family structures, clear and honest dialogue is key. Stepparents need to communicate openly about their role, expectations, and boundaries, allowing stepchildren to express their feelings without fear of judgment. By establishing a safe space for open discussions, you will strengthen your ability to relate to one another.

Building a strong family connection is all about mutual respect. It's not just about tolerating differences but appreciating them—embracing the quirks, opinions, and boundaries that make each family member unique. In blended families, understanding and valuing your stepchild's individuality is so crucial. It's a delicate balance of respecting the existing parent-child relationship while also nurturing your own connection in its own right. Think of it as a two-way street where both sides acknowledge and appreciate each other's roles for a smoother ride.

Feeling a sense of belonging is crucial for a tight-knit family, especially in non-traditional setups. Stepparents can actively include their stepchildren in family activities and decisions, making them an integral part of the unit. Imagine creating new traditions that reflect everyone's interests and viewpoints. It's like weaving a tapestry of shared experiences where each family member feels not just noticed but genuinely valued. Remember, this approach can help the child successfully navigate future relationships.

Flexibility is the secret sauce for maintaining a strong family bond, especially in your blended family. Picture it like a dance where roles, routines, and expectations are fluid and everyone is joining in the fun. Stepparents and stepchildren are like dance partners, learning and adjusting to each other's needs and preferences. It's this flexibility that keeps the family resilient and moving with the rhythm of life. Adapting to the ever-changing dynamics is like a family superpower.

Creating strong family ties is like planting seeds that need time and care to grow. In non-traditional families, especially those with step-relationships, it's a journey that demands patience and dedication. Step into your role with a sprinkle of empathy, and remember that bonding with stepchildren is a gradual process. On the other hand, keep in mind that at times your stepchild may need a bit of space and time to find their rhythm in the new family groove. They have gone through many changes; it is only natural that they will need even more time to evolve and grow into the new family flow. It's all about investing time and effort in letting connections bloom naturally, like a garden that flourishes over time.

As you read through this chapter, keep in mind that a rock-solid family connection goes beyond traditional boundaries; it thrives on trust, communication, mutual respect, inclusivity, adaptability, dedication, and support. When it comes to step-relationships, nurturing these qualities becomes the heart of building resilient and loving family bonds. Understanding the unique dynamics and investing in trust, communication, and mutual respect lays the foundation for a family bond that's not just strong but also deeply fulfilling. You are building YOUR family!

Celebrate Their Unique Strengths

Acknowledging and celebrating the strengths and achievements of your stepchild plays a pivotal role in shaping their self-esteem and creating a positive family environment. It's about recognizing their unique abilities, efforts, and milestones, irrespective of their nature, and expressing genuine appreciation for all that they do. Consider a scenario where your stepchild exhibits exceptional creativity in art. Acknowledging this talent and proudly displaying their artwork at home on the refrigerator, or perhaps even framed on the wall, becomes a powerful affirmation of their skills. Sometimes non-verbal gestures such as these can have even more impact than a traditional congratulatory response. However, it's not merely about showcasing their work but conveying that their talents are recognized and valued within their family.

Encouraging their interests and passions is equally vital so they feel empowered to continue pursuing their dreams and aspirations. When you actively support their pursuits, whether it's enrolling them in activities they enjoy or providing resources for their hobbies, you show genuine interest in their growth. If your stepchild expresses a keen interest in music, offering them opportunities like music classes or providing musical instruments reflects your investment in nurturing their talents. Even letting them pick the playlist for the morning's commute can affirm that you think they have good taste in music.

Acknowledging their achievements, no matter how small, is the basis of building their self-worth. Recognizing their determination in overcoming challenges or commending their empathy towards others cultivates a positive atmosphere. This celebration of their efforts creates an environment where they feel seen and valued, fostering a sense of pride in their accomplishments. Also, be sure to share these moments with your spouse. There is no better way to strengthen your marriage than by showing how devoted and proud you are of their child.

Moreover, integrating their strengths and achievements into family activities further reinforces their sense of worth. Organizing events where they can showcase their talents—such as performing a musical piece or exhibiting their artwork at a family dinner or gathering—allows them to feel acknowledged and appreciated by the entire family. This recognition not only boosts their confidence but also solidifies their sense of belonging within the family unit. If they have the self-assurance to perform in front of the family unit, imagine how they will be able to perform outside of it. You are becoming a key part of your child's ability to succeed in the real world.

Be Unified with All Parents

Creating a harmonious environment involves unity among all parental figures within the family. Collaborating with biological parents, stepparents, and all involved parties establishes a consistent approach to parenting that the child can depend on. It is this steadiness that allows them to self-regulate, regardless of whether they are a CD, Straddler, or MY personality. We all crave stability. Having open discussions or family meetings where all parents align on household rules, expectations, and disciplinary strategies ensures a unified front. Consistency in rules like bedtime routines or guidelines for screen time across households minimizes confusion and offers stability for your stepchild. They will feel safe.

It's not just about agreeing on rules but also about presenting a united front when it comes to acknowledging and appreciating your stepchild's strengths and achievements. Celebrating these milestones together as a unified parental unit reinforces the message that their successes are valued and supported by everyone involved in their life no matter what. This unity not only fosters a cohesive family environment but also strengthens the bond between you and your stepchild, establishing a foundation built on trust, appreciation, and shared values.

Consistency in parenting approaches across households is instrumental in reducing potential conflicts for children in blended families. When rules, expectations, and disciplinary strategies align between households, it creates a seamless transition for the child. For instance, if one household has specific guidelines about homework or screen time, maintaining these consistent rules when the child moves to the other household helps in reinforcing stability and clarity for the child, preventing confusion or conflicts.

Open and transparent communication among parental figures is the cornerstone of maintaining this consistency. Establishing channels where all parents can openly discuss and understand each other's parenting styles and decisions is crucial. Regular discussions about household rules, changes in routines, or adjustments in disciplinary strategies ensure that everyone involved is on the same page. For instance, if there are changes in routines or disciplinary methods in one household, communicating these adjustments to all parental figures helps in maintaining a unified approach.

Moreover, demonstrating mutual respect and support for each other's role as parents is vital in fostering a healthy family dynamic. It's essential to acknowledge and appreciate each other's contributions to parenting regardless of biological relationships. This appreciation creates an atmosphere of collaboration and understanding. When all parental figures support one another, it reinforces the idea that they're working towards the same goal: the well-being and development of the child.

Consistency also involves finding a balance between flexibility and adherence to established rules. While it's crucial to maintain coherence in parenting approaches, it's equally important to allow flexibility in certain situations. Understanding that different households might have unique dynamics and being open to accommodating reasonable adjustments can contribute to a more harmonious co-parenting environment.

Implementing strategies like shared calendars, a shared document or family organization app, or written agreements about certain rules and expectations can also help in maximizing consistency. This ensures that everyone involved, including the child, is aware of the guidelines and routines. For instance, a shared schedule can detail important routines like bedtime or mealtime, creating consistency for the child between households. You could also create a platform for all of the adults in the child's life to provide feedback and notes on what is happening that week for all to refer to.

Furthermore, recognizing and addressing any conflicts or discrepancies in parenting styles promptly is essential. There is no time like the present! Avoiding conflicts requires a willingness to compromise, understand different perspectives, and work together to find solutions that serve the child's best interests. It might involve mediation or seeking professional guidance to navigate disagreements and ensure a consistent and supportive environment for the child.

Ultimately, a unified and consistent approach to parenting between households ensures that the child understands and follows similar rules and expectations regardless of where they are, allowing them to thrive in an environment that prioritizes their well-being and development. It is all about clear expectations!

Show Them How to Handle Conflicts

Healthy conflict resolution is an invaluable skill, and modeling this behavior within a blended family can have a profound impact on your stepchild's development—especially after what may have been a challenging transition for the family to get to where you are today.

Let's dive into a story about Mark, a stepfather, and his stepdaughter, Emily. They had differing opinions on how to organize household chores. Instead of letting the disagreement escalate, Mark calmly initiated a conversation. He listened to Emily's perspective, validating her concerns about feeling overwhelmed by the chores on top of her homework. Through empathetic listening, they found a compromise that made chores more manageable for Emily without overburdening her.

Another example of modeling healthy conflict resolution involves demonstrating empathy and understanding. Consider the scenario of Sarah, a stepmother, and her stepson, Jake, who had differing opinions on how to balance time between schoolwork and extracurricular activities.

Sarah acknowledged Jake's passion for hockey and piano lessons but also emphasized the importance of academics, specifically bringing up his grades in mathematics. By empathizing with Jake's enthusiasm for his chosen passions while also highlighting the significance of a balanced approach, Sarah showcased the value of considering multiple viewpoints in conflict resolution. They problem-solved together, integrating ways to better understand mathematical concepts that were troubling him with piano theory and hockey plays. He was thrilled she took the time to think outside the penalty box!

Encouraging open discussions about conflicts is crucial. For example, after resolving a disagreement about a family outing, Sam, a stepfather, initiated a family conversation. They openly discussed differing preferences and devised a plan that accommodated everyone's interests. This practice of discussing conflicts and their resolutions not only demonstrates effective conflict resolution strategies but also fosters an environment where conflicts are addressed openly and constructively.

Moreover, demonstrating patience and a solution-oriented approach during conflicts significantly influences a stepchild's perspective. Imagine a situation where Jane, a stepmother, and her stepdaughter, Lily, disagreed about screen time limits. Instead of a confrontation, Jane patiently listened to Lily's concerns about feeling restricted. Together, they devised a screen time schedule that balanced Lily's desires with healthy limits. This approach emphasized problem-solving and patience rather than conflict escalation.

Teaching by example is crucial, and it's not just about resolving conflicts but about the process itself. Demonstrating calmness, active listening, and a focus on solutions during disagreements—like Julia, a stepmother, did when addressing a disagreement about family outings—showcases a positive conflict resolution model. By remaining composed and redirecting the discussion toward finding common ground, Julia instilled the importance of maintaining a constructive approach to resolving conflicts within the family.

Consistently exhibiting these behaviors offers a blueprint for handling disagreements. A stepchild observing a stepparent navigate conflicts with patience, empathy, and a focus on solutions learns the importance of effective communication and compromise. It creates an environment where conflicts are seen as opportunities for growth and understanding, laying the groundwork for a healthier and more harmonious family dynamic throughout their lives.

Recognize and Validate Their Feelings Through Check-Ins

Regularly checking in with your stepchild to acknowledge and validate their feelings is a fundamental aspect of fostering the safe and supportive environment within your blended family you so wish to establish. Initiating conversations that invite them to express their emotions demonstrates your genuine interest in their well-being. Utilizing simple yet meaningful inquiries like "How are you feeling today?" or "Is there anything on your mind?" during casual interactions provides them with opportunities to share their thoughts and emotions. For example, asking about their day at school or inquiring about their hobbies can organically transition into deeper conversations about their feelings or concerns. Maybe they saw something on TV earlier in the week they didn't understand and have been waiting for the right moment to ask someone about it. You can be that person for them.

Establishing a routine for these check-ins contributes to a sense of reliability and comfort for your stepchild. Designating a specific time each week for a one-on-one conversation or check-in session conveys that you prioritize their feelings and are consistently available to listen whenever they need you. This regularity in providing them with a platform to express themselves nurtures trust and openness in your relationship, creating a space where they feel comfortable sharing their thoughts. They will know they can depend on you in most everyday situations. Imagine how they will feel when times are difficult!

Active listening plays a pivotal role during these check-ins. It goes beyond merely hearing their words; it involves understanding the emotions underlying their expressions. Encouraging them to articulate their feelings without judgment or interruption allows them to feel heard and validated. For instance, if they express concerns about a school assignment, actively listening and acknowledging their stress by saying, "It sounds like you're feeling overwhelmed. How can I help?" demonstrates your support and willingness to address their emotional needs.

Make sure when doing these check-ins that the cell phone is out of reach and the television is off. In a time where screens and distractions are everywhere, it is even more important to be present for your stepchild.

Responding empathetically to their emotions also reinforces a sense of understanding and support. Validating their feelings through expressions of empathy and understanding, such as saying, "I can understand why that would make you feel that way," assures them that their emotions are not only recognized but also accepted. This affirmation encourages them to continue sharing their thoughts and feelings openly, strengthening the bond between you and your stepchild.

Incorporating empathy into your responses demonstrates a deep understanding of their perspective. By acknowledging their emotions without judgment, you create an environment where they feel safe expressing themselves. For example, if they express frustration about a friend-related issue, respond with empathy by saying, "It sounds like you're going through a tough time with your friend. How can we work through this together?" This conveys your commitment to supporting them emotionally.

Asking more specific questions during check-ins can delve into their emotional well-being as well as validate their situation. For instance, inquire about their favorite and least favorite parts of the day, what aspects of a situation made them happy or upset, or if there's anything they wish to think about a little more deeply. These targeted questions can guide the conversation toward their emotions and provide them with a structured space to express themselves.

Additionally, sharing your own experiences or emotions can create a more reciprocal and open atmosphere. They will be able to see you as YOU, not just another adult in their life. Offering personal anecdotes or expressing how you navigate challenging emotions helps normalize the idea of discussing feelings. For example, sharing a story about how you coped with stress at work can pave the way for them to share their own stressors.

To recap, remember that regular check-ins that prioritize emotional well-being contribute significantly to the health and strength of your relationship with your stepchild. Through consistent and empathetic communication, you create a foundation of trust and understanding, fostering an environment where they feel valued and supported in expressing their emotions.

Model Emotional Regulation

Modeling emotional regulation is more than just a lesson; it's a guiding principle for your stepchild in navigating their own emotional landscape effectively. It's about demonstrating how to handle stress, disappointment, or frustration in a composed manner, setting a positive example for them to follow. When facing challenging situations, maintaining composure and handling disagreements calmly and respectfully are demonstrations of effective emotional regulation. For instance, if a discussion becomes heated, pausing to gather thoughts before responding showcases the importance of managing emotions in conflicts and shows that it's okay to take a moment to think before reacting.

Keep in mind that while this process is to help you effectively love your stepchild, it is about so much more. This process can help you grow as well. Moreover, by modeling these good behaviors more consciously, you may end up embracing a new idea of mindfulness in your own headspace.

Sharing personal experiences where you've successfully regulated your emotions can be incredibly insightful for your stepchild. Narrating instances when you managed your frustration or stress effectively and the positive outcomes that followed provides tangible examples. For example, recounting a time when a stressful situation was resolved calmly and productively can illustrate the benefits of emotional regulation. These stories offer practical insights for your stepchild, enabling them to comprehend the real impact of regulating emotions in everyday life.

Moreover, it's important to highlight the tangible benefits of emotional regulation. Explaining how handling emotions calmly leads to better decision-making and improved relationships helps your stepchild understand its significance. Too often as adults we bark directives at children, of course for their wellbeing but without proper explanation. Discussing how managing frustration helped in finding constructive solutions or improved communication during conflicts emphasizes the positive outcomes of emotional regulation, making it relatable and applicable.

In addition to discussing the benefits, providing guidance on specific strategies for emotional regulation can be highly beneficial. Teaching techniques like deep breathing exercises, mindfulness practices, or the importance of taking a moment to reflect before reacting equips them with practical tools to manage their emotions effectively. For instance, suggesting a relaxation technique during moments of stress, or encouraging them to take a break when feeling overwhelmed, empowers them with coping mechanisms they can implement in their daily life. Think about what coping strategies work for you, and consider a way to share them with your stepchild or scaffold them so they can incorporate them into their daily life.

Encouraging them to identify emotions and express them in healthy ways is also crucial. Helping them label their emotions, whether frustration, sadness, or excitement, allows them to recognize and manage these feelings. Creating a safe space where they feel comfortable expressing their emotions without judgment or criticism fosters emotional intelligence and resilience.

Furthermore, demonstrating your own vulnerability by admitting when you struggle with emotions and how you work through them can be impactful. Sharing that everyone experiences difficult emotions and that it's okay to seek help or take time to process feelings encourages them to embrace their emotional journey.

Consistently reinforcing these lessons through everyday interactions and being patient as they learn to regulate their emotions is vital. It is too easy to fly off the handle on hard days, perhaps responding in a way that is not kind or empathetic. In these moments, own your shortcomings and pivot. Encourage them when they handle emotions well and offer guidance when they struggle, emphasizing that learning to manage emotions is a continuous and challenging process.

In essence, modeling emotional regulation isn't just about displaying control over emotions; it's about teaching resilience, empathy, and the ability to navigate life's challenges effectively. Through your example and guidance, you're providing your stepchild with essential tools that will help them thrive emotionally and build stronger relationships throughout their life.

Chapter Six

Establishing Healthy Boundaries

Before we look at how to establish boundaries with your stepchild, let's talk a little bit about what boundaries are and why they are so important. Setting boundaries in interpersonal relationships defines the limits, expectations, and parameters within a relationship. It involves establishing guidelines and rules that govern how individuals interact, communicate, and behave with each other. These boundaries are crucial as they delineate one's personal space, emotional needs, and autonomy, safeguarding individuals from being overwhelmed, manipulated, or disrespected in relationships.

Boundaries are the invisible lines that demarcate the physical, emotional, and psychological limits individuals set to protect their well-being and preserve their identity within relationships. They signify the personal space and limits we establish in various aspects of our lives, such as physical boundaries (personal space, touch), emotional boundaries (feelings, self-worth), mental boundaries (thoughts, beliefs), and even spiritual boundaries (values, faith). While exact boundaries may differ from person to person, the essence of boundaries is rooted in respect for the person and their autonomy. Where an MY may enjoy physical signs of affection and interaction, a CD may be more reserved. Regardless of the exact line, the boundary must be respected and safety for the child is key above all.

The importance of setting boundaries truly cannot be overstated. Boundaries serve as a protective mechanism, safeguarding individuals from experiencing emotional exhaustion, manipulation, and abuse. They act as a form of self-care, ensuring that individuals prioritize their mental and emotional health within relationships. Healthy boundaries foster mutual respect, trust, and understanding between individuals, laying the foundation for healthy and fulfilling relationships. Boundaries create clear expectations and mitigate abuse when heeded.

Without boundaries, relationships risk becoming codependent or toxic. Codependency refers to a dynamic where one or both individuals rely excessively on the other for their sense of identity, self-worth, and emotional fulfillment. It often involves a lack of boundaries, leading to blurred lines between individuals' thoughts, emotions, and actions. In a codependent relationship, there's an imbalance where one person's needs take precedence over the other's, leading to an unhealthy dependency that can hinder personal growth and autonomy.

On the other hand, toxic relationships are characterized by patterns of behavior that are emotionally or psychologically damaging. Without boundaries, individuals might experience manipulation, emotional abuse, or neglect within such relationships. Toxic relationships can erode self-esteem, create stress, and contribute to mental health issues.

Setting boundaries in relationships involves clear and effective communication. It means expressing your needs, limits, and expectations openly and assertively. For instance, communicating the need for personal space or privacy, establishing limits on what is acceptable behavior, or setting expectations regarding communication frequency are ways to define boundaries.

It's essential to recognize that setting boundaries is not about controlling or manipulating others. Instead, it's about respecting oneself and others. Healthy boundaries respect individual autonomy, allowing each person to have their own opinions, feelings, and space within the relationship. They create a balanced dynamic where both individual's needs and emotions are acknowledged and honored. A respectful person will never question your boundaries; remember that.

A lack of boundaries can lead to various issues within relationships. For instance, without clear boundaries, individuals might feel suffocated, overwhelmed, or taken advantage of. This can result in resentment, conflicts, or emotional distance. Boundaries act as a preventive measure against these problems, helping maintain harmony, respect, and understanding between partners.

Moreover, boundaries are a crucial aspect of self-care. They enable individuals to prioritize their mental, emotional, and physical well-being. By setting limits on what is acceptable or unacceptable behavior, individuals protect themselves from being mistreated or exploited within relationships. This self-respect forms the foundation for healthy and fulfilling connections.

Setting boundaries in interpersonal relationships involves defining and communicating personal limits, needs, and expectations. It's a fundamental aspect of fostering healthy connections and safeguarding individuals from codependency and toxicity within relationships. Boundaries protect emotional well-being, promote mutual respect, and enable individuals to maintain a sense of identity and autonomy within their interactions with others.

Create Boundaries With Your Stepchild

Establishing clear boundaries with your stepchild is pivotal not only for nurturing a healthy and respectful relationship within your blended family but also beyond. These boundaries form the framework for mutual respect, understanding, and household expectations. Consider starting conversations about boundaries by emphasizing mutual respect and setting examples. You might say, "I respect your space and privacy, and I hope you can extend the same courtesy. Let's discuss how we can ensure everyone feels comfortable at home."

Consistency is key in boundary enforcement. Once boundaries are set, it's crucial to maintain them consistently. For instance, if you've agreed on specific rules about screen time or curfew, ensure these regulations are consistently upheld. Consistency provides stability and predictability, helping your stepchild understand the expectations and feel secure in their environment.

Communicating these boundaries respectfully is equally essential. Explain the rationale behind certain rules, such as screen time limitations, emphasizing the balance between leisure activities and responsibilities. You can approach it by saying, "We set these limits because we believe it's important to have a balance between fun and responsibilities like homework and family time."

Encouraging open communication when setting boundaries is beneficial. Involve your stepchild in the process by discussing and negotiating certain household rules together. This involvement allows them to feel heard and valued, fostering a sense of ownership within the family dynamics. For instance, when discussing chores or study hours, invite their input: "What do you think would be a fair way for us to divide up household chores?" You are teaching them to define their boundaries and also articulate them!

It's also crucial to create space for feedback. Let your stepchild know that their thoughts and opinions matter. By continuing to actively listen and acknowledge their perspective, you create an atmosphere of respect and understanding. You could initiate the above conversation by saying, "I value your thoughts on our household rules. Is there anything you feel we could adjust or discuss together?" before defining the boundary.

Remember, setting boundaries isn't about control but about mutual respect and establishing a harmonious living environment. By approaching boundary discussions with respect, consistency, rationale, and openness to dialogue, you foster an atmosphere that encourages mutual understanding and respect within your blended family. Everyone has a voice at the table.

Give Them Space

Respecting your stepchild's need for personal space is an integral part of nurturing a healthy relationship built on trust and mutual understanding and is so important in your unique family dynamic. Acknowledging and honoring their need for both physical and emotional space is vital for their emotional well-being and development, especially in a period of accelerated change or development. This space provides them the freedom to explore their identity, interests, and emotions without feeling intruded upon.

For instance, granting them dedicated time and physical privacy in their room allows them to unwind, pursue hobbies, or reflect without feeling constantly observed or interrupted. This autonomy fosters a sense of independence and self-discovery, enabling them to cultivate their individuality. Providing emotional space also involves giving them room to express their emotions without feeling pressured to do so. It's essential to create an environment where they feel comfortable sharing their feelings but also respected when they choose to keep them private. Of course, this approach must be approached individually should this be a safety issue for a young child or with particular challenges.

Balancing this need for space with maintaining open communication is crucial. Encouraging periodic check-ins to understand how they're feeling or what they're interested in without prying into personal matters demonstrates a balance between respecting their privacy and showing genuine interest in their well-being. For instance, asking them about their day or what they're passionate about opens avenues for conversation without intruding into personal space.

Additionally, recognizing and responding to cues indicating their need for space is equally important. If they withdraw or seek solitude, respecting their choice without pressing for information or engagement communicates your understanding and respect for their boundaries. This understanding fosters trust and demonstrates your commitment to supporting their autonomy and individuality within the family dynamic. However, if you ever feel their safety or well-being is in question, be sure to approach them without judgment or speak to your spouse about the best ways to support the child.

Creating an environment where boundaries are respected not only encourages a healthy sense of self but also strengthens the trust between you and your stepchild. This respect for their need for personal space allows for a balanced relationship where they feel both supported and free to explore their individuality.

Foster Their Hunger for Adventure

Variety is the spice of life! Encouraging and nurturing your stepchild's adventurous spirit is a pivotal part of their personal development and growth. Supporting their inclination towards exploration, whether it's trying new activities, visiting new places, or engaging in learning experiences fosters their curiosity and helps them develop valuable life skills. We all have that *thing* that ignites our spirit. Make sure to find theirs!

One way to foster this adventurous spirit is by planning family outings to explore different places. Whether it's visiting local landmarks, hiking trails, museums, or even planning a family trip to a new city or country, these experiences expose them to diverse cultures, perspectives, and environments. For instance, organizing a weekend camping trip or a visit to a historical site not only nurtures their curiosity but also creates lasting memories and strengthens family bonds.

Moreover, encouraging them to try out different hobbies or activities contributes to their personal growth. Whether it's joining a sports team, trying art classes, or learning a musical instrument, these experiences help them discover their interests and talents. For instance, supporting their decision to join a drama club or encouraging them to learn coding taps into their potential and broadens their horizons.

Incorporating learning experiences into everyday activities also fosters their sense of adventure. For instance, turning routine grocery shopping into a learning opportunity by exploring new cuisines or teaching them about budgeting and decision-making in real-life situations can be both educational and adventurous. It encourages them to approach everyday tasks with curiosity and a willingness to learn.

Most importantly, fostering their adventurous spirit requires creating an environment where taking risks and exploring new possibilities is encouraged and supported. This could involve providing positive reinforcement when they step out of their comfort zone (especially for a CD personality type), praising their efforts in trying new things, and showing appreciation for their willingness to explore. These actions not only boost their confidence but also instill in them a sense of resilience and adaptability, essential traits for navigating life's challenges.

Respect Their Needs and Wants

Respecting your stepchild's needs and desires is fundamental in fostering a harmonious and respectful relationship. Acknowledging their preferences and considering their opinions in family decisions is a powerful way to validate their feelings and promote open communication. For instance, suppose they express a preference for certain activities like hiking or visiting a museum. In that case, making plans to accommodate these interests within the family's schedule demonstrates your respect for their individuality and encourages them to express their preferences confidently. They will know that you see them for who they are!

Listening actively to their desires and opinions, and incorporating them into family decisions when possible, affirms their sense of value within the family unit. Whether it's selecting a restaurant for a family dinner or planning a weekend activity, involving them in the decision-making process conveys that their thoughts matter and are taken seriously. If you are not able to accommodate their preferences, be sure to acknowledge that too. They will know that you are present and that you care.

In keeping with this, it's so crucial to balance this with practicality and reason. While accommodating their preferences within reasonable limits is important, it's equally vital to explain certain constraints or limitations that may impact decisions. For instance, if the family is planning a budget-friendly outing, discussing the options available within the budget and collectively deciding on the best choice helps them understand the considerations involved in decision-making.

Moreover, demonstrating flexibility and openness to their suggestions, even if some cannot be immediately fulfilled, encourages that ongoing stream of communication. Again, if their desires cannot be accommodated at a specific moment due to constraints, discussing alternative options or planning for future opportunities showcases your willingness to consider their preferences and creates an environment where open communication is encouraged.

Overall, by respecting and acknowledging your stepchild's needs and desires, you not only validate their feelings but also nurture an atmosphere of mutual respect and understanding within the family. This practice encourages healthy communication, fosters their confidence in expressing themselves, and reinforces their sense of belonging in the family unit.

Ask Before Giving Advice

Think before you speak! Respecting your stepchild's autonomy in decision-making is another key facet of fostering a healthy and respectful dynamic. Let's delve into the tale of Tom, a stepfather navigating the delicate balance of offering guidance to his stepson, Max. When Max faced challenges with schoolwork, Tom recognized the importance of treading lightly. Not doing well in school was a sensitive topic for Tom when he was young, too. He knew jumping in with unsolicited advice might not be well-received or helpful. Instead, Tom approached Max with a question: "Would you like some ideas on how to tackle this assignment?" This simple question honored Max's autonomy and allowed him to decide whether he wanted Tom's input. Max appreciated the respect for his space, and when he agreed to Tom's guidance, the conversation flowed more smoothly.

Creating an environment where your stepchild feels empowered to make their own choices is essential. Let's consider Rachel, a stepmother who realized this when her stepdaughter, Oona, faced friendship issues. As with Tom, Rachel could recall the difficulties of navigating these relationships as an adolescent. Rather than imposing her advice as an authoritarian, Rachel gently asked, "Are you open to hearing how I dealt with a similar situation when I was your age?" This approach respected Lily's autonomy while offering support. Lily felt heard and appreciated Rachel's willingness to share her experiences without forcing her opinions.

Conversation Starters

- "I noticed you're dealing with [specific issue]. Would you like some advice or help navigating this? I've been thinking about you a lot lately."

- "When I faced a similar situation, I did [describe your experience]. If you're interested, I'm happy to share. These things aren't always easy and it's good to have someone to talk to."

- "I'm here if you need guidance or suggestions, but only if you feel comfortable discussing it. Our conversation is on your terms."

- "Can I offer some thoughts on this situation, or would you prefer to handle it on your own?"

- "I respect your judgment, but if you ever need a sounding board, I'm always here to listen, and I love you."

This respectful approach not only allows the stepchild to retain control over their decisions but also communicates that their opinions and choices matter. It creates an open dialogue that is not forced or one-sided. It fosters an environment of mutual respect and trust. By seeking consent before offering guidance, you're setting the stage for more open and constructive communication. It encourages a collaborative problem-solving approach where both parties contribute to the conversation, leading to more meaningful and supportive interactions. Ultimately, this practice strengthens the bond and nurtures trust, fostering a relationship built on respect and understanding.

Chapter Seven
Have Fun

In some ways, this may be the most important chapter. You have done the hard work, and while life is full of challenges, it is oh so full of rewards and good times. Think of the memories that will warm your hearts on cold evenings as you get older. Consider how you both will feel, looking back on that special road trip or the time you tripped and fell at the mall. These moments will be special and important for one reason: they are yours.

Having fun with family members is an essential aspect of nurturing strong bonds and creating lasting memories. However, the definition of "fun" can vary widely among different family members, particularly in non-traditional scenarios involving stepchildren and stepparents. Understanding these differences and embracing diverse perspectives on what constitutes fun is crucial in fostering inclusive and enjoyable experiences that strengthen family relationships.

Fun serves as a universal language that bridges gaps and promotes bonding, especially within blended families. It's an avenue for shared experiences and laughter, fostering an environment of joy and relaxation. One of the key challenges in non-traditional family settings is this diverse understanding of fun among different family members. What might be enjoyable for one individual could be vastly different for another. For instance, a stepparent might have a different idea of fun, perhaps involving outdoor adventures or cultural experiences, while a stepchild might prefer activities related to technology or creative arts. Recognizing and appreciating these differences allows families to explore a diverse range of activities that cater to everyone's interests. Remember, there is something for everyone!

Variety in the definition of fun also contributes to a richer tapestry of experiences within a family. Don't be afraid to shake things up a bit. In blended families, encouraging open discussions about preferences and interests helps in planning activities that cater to different tastes. For example, organizing a weekend where each family member gets to pick an activity or outing ensures that everyone feels included and has a chance to engage in something they enjoy.

Engaging in activities that appeal to different family members' notions of fun promotes inclusivity and strengthens relationships. Stepparents and stepchildren bonding over activities they both enjoy—whether it's trying out new dance moves from the internet, exploring nature, or playing video games—creates opportunities for shared experiences. These moments of shared enjoyment help break down barriers, fostering understanding and a sense of unity within the family. Sometimes, there is no better bonding than working together to complete a delicious brownie recipe!

Fun serves as a catalyst for creating relaxed and comfortable environments within the family. In non-traditional family dynamics, it can aid in easing potential tensions and uncertainties. Stepparents can use fun activities as a means to connect with stepchildren in a relaxed setting, fostering a sense of trust and comfort. Similarly, stepchildren can use shared moments of enjoyment to build rapport with their stepparents, creating a space where relationships can thrive. This should be a give and take.

Moreover, fun-filled activities contribute to creating lasting memories. In non-traditional families, these shared memories are instrumental in solidifying bonds. Whether it's a day trip, a movie night, a creative project, or a sports activity, these experiences become touchstones in the family's collective history, strengthening the connection between stepparents and stepchildren. Be sure to savor those moments. If you are having a great excursion as a family, buy a Christmas ornament to hang on your tree for years to come so when you look at it you feel connected to that core moment. If you are enjoying a particular movie at the theater and the whole family enjoyed it, consider buying a memento or the digital copy when it is out for release so you can relive the fun. Fun should be a recurring practice.

The significance of fun in family dynamics extends beyond mere enjoyment. It's about fostering an environment where individuals feel heard, valued, and included. Respect is fun! Acknowledging and embracing the unique interests and preferences of stepchildren communicates acceptance and appreciation. Simultaneously, stepchildren recognizing and engaging in activities that their stepparents enjoy demonstrate a willingness to build a relationship based on mutual respect and understanding.

Let's remember that embracing diverse definitions of fun, planning activities that cater to different interests, and cherishing shared moments of enjoyment contribute significantly to building harmonious and enduring relationships within the family. It's your family; time to start enjoying it!

Do Activities They Will Enjoy

Initiating discussions in a relaxed setting, such as during meal times, before bed, during bath time, or while engaging in casual activities, can be an effective way to learn about your stepchild's interests. You might consider sharing your own hobbies or experiences first, creating a safe space for them to reciprocate and add their own take. This approach allows them to see that you're open to sharing and encourages them to discuss their interests comfortably. For example, while preparing dinner together, you could chat about your favorite hobbies or pastimes and then inquire about theirs in a non-intrusive manner.

Expressing genuine curiosity and actively listening when they speak about their interests is crucial. Avoid interrupting or steering the conversation toward your own experiences; instead, focus on what they're sharing. Ask follow-up questions to delve deeper into their hobbies or passions. For instance, if they mention a particular activity they enjoy, inquire about what specifically draws them to it or what they find fascinating about it. As always, make sure to put the phone down and take the headphones out of your ears. The child is your focus!

Demonstrate your support by giving them the opportunity to pick activities or outings related to their interests or something they have been curious about. Encourage them to choose an activity for the family to do together, or suggest an event they might want to attend. For instance, if they're into art, propose a visit to an art exhibit or suggest an arts and crafts session at home. This shows that you value their interests and are willing to engage with them in activities that matter to them. Let them have the opportunity to be the expert in your fun—let them guide the way.

Avoid judgment or criticism about their hobbies even if their interests differ from yours. We do not all enjoy the same things, and that is one of the great joys of life in celebrating differences. Embrace their unique passions and let them know that their preferences are respected and valued. This inclusivity and acceptance foster an environment where they feel comfortable sharing their interests without fear of judgment. You like them for who they are, not for their likes or interests.

Create a dedicated space within the home that reflects their interests. It could be a corner of the living room for their hobby-related items or a shelf to display things they've made or collected in the entryway to show to all who enter. This gesture not only acknowledges their passions but also encourages conversations about their interests.

If your stepchild has specific talents or skills, continue to encourage and celebrate their accomplishments. Praise their efforts and achievements in their hobbies or passions. For example, if they're talented in a particular sport or artistic endeavor, attend their games or exhibitions and express pride in their achievements. This affirmation helps build their confidence and reinforces their trust in sharing their interests with you.

Lastly, be patient and understanding. Some stepchildren might take time to feel comfortable sharing their interests, especially if they've faced challenges in expressing themselves in the past. Give them the space and time they need, and let the relationship develop organically. As they feel more secure and accepted, they'll likely open up and share more about their interests with you.

Encourage Them to Spend Time With Their Entire Family

Encouraging your stepchild to join family activities requires a delicate balance between fostering inclusion and respecting their autonomy. We don't want to do everything all the time! There are many ebbs and flows to these interactions, and fun cannot be forced. One way to approach this is by making invitations open and inviting without applying any pressure. Express enthusiasm about upcoming family events or activities and extend a casual invitation without making it obligatory. For example, mention an upcoming family game night or a day trip to the zoo and ask if they would like to join in. This approach keeps the invitation inclusive and non-confrontational, allowing them the freedom to decide.

Creating a routine for family activities can also help normalize spending time together and make it a healthy routine. Establishing a regular slot, like a weekly movie night, a monthly outing, or a Sunday brunch gives everyone something to look forward to and reduces any awkwardness associated with the invitation. When these activities become part of the family's routine, they can naturally integrate into your stepchild's schedule without feeling forced.

Continuing to involve your stepchild in the decision-making process regarding family activities can be empowering. Always ask for their input when planning outings or events. Seek their preferences and consider their suggestions when organizing family gatherings. This collaborative approach allows them to feel heard, valued, and an active participant in family decisions, making them more likely to engage willingly in these activities.

Integrating their interests into family activities can create a more welcoming atmosphere. For instance, if your stepchild has a particular hobby or enjoys specific activities, try to incorporate those into family time. This not only allows them to share their interests but also makes them feel understood and appreciated within the family setting. It could be as simple as suggesting a movie they love for the family movie night or planning an outing related to their hobbies.

Ensuring flexibility in participation is also crucial. While encouraging their involvement, acknowledge and respect their boundaries or personal preferences. Let them know that they are welcome to join but also assure them that it's okay if they prefer to opt out for any reason. This approach helps in avoiding any feelings of obligation and fosters an environment where they feel comfortable and respected.

Modeling enthusiasm and genuine interest in family activities can be contagious. Show excitement and eagerness when planning or participating in family events. Your positive attitude and engagement can influence their perception and encourage them to join in without feeling awkward or hesitant. You want to be one of their biggest fans!

Creating a relaxed and inviting atmosphere during family gatherings is key to making them more appealing to your stepchild. Encourage open conversations, foster a sense of humor, and allow space for casual interaction among family members. When everyone feels comfortable and at ease, it becomes more natural for your stepchild to participate without feeling awkward or out of place.

Lastly, celebrate moments of togetherness and express appreciation for their participation. It may not always be comfortable, but be sure to involve all the adults in the child's life when it matters most. Let them know that the adults will show up for them no matter their own situations. Acknowledge and express gratitude for their involvement in those family activities. Positive reinforcement and recognition of their contributions can encourage their continued engagement and make family time more enjoyable for everyone.

Build a Friendship

Building a genuine friendship with your stepchild is a journey that thrives on investment and sincerity. If you have taken the sentiments of this book to heart, it should be at least starting to grow organically and of its own accord. It's about more than cohabiting; it's about creating an atmosphere of comfort. One approach is to carve out dedicated time for open, heart-to-heart conversations. Sharing your own life stories and experiences, along with a genuine interest in theirs, establishes a bridge of understanding. Imagine a scenario where your stepchild, Emily, expresses an interest in writing. By sharing your own journey as an aspiring writer, you not only bond over a shared passion but also provide inspiration and guidance, fostering a deeper connection. Treat your stepchild how you would want to be treated.

Express genuine interest in their world—be curious about their interests, hobbies, and experiences. Cultivate an environment of non-judgmental listening, creating space for them to share freely. Dive into topics they're passionate about, whether it's music, trends, or current events. Emphasizing relatable moments while acknowledging differences can break down barriers and foster a relatable connection.

Active participation in their interests is a powerful method to nurture camaraderie. Engage in their hobbies, whether it's gaming, a TV show, or a social media platform. Offer to play a game together or binge-watch a series they enjoy. This shared involvement displays a genuine interest in their world and establishes shared experiences that bridge the generational gap. For instance, suggesting a movie night where both of you take turns picking films opens avenues for conversation and mutual enjoyment.

Moreover, embrace and celebrate their passions and achievements wholeheartedly. Attend their performances, matches, or presentations to exhibit your support and excitement. Celebrating their victories, irrespective of size, fortifies your bond and underscores your investment in their happiness. For example, attending an art exhibition showcasing their work amplifies their confidence and highlights your support for their talents.

Navigating the generational gap requires providing guidance and support without being intrusive. Help when they face challenges but respect their space to seek advice if needed. For instance, if they're struggling with schoolwork, extend your help in a non-imposing manner. A gentle assurance like, "I'm available if you need assistance," communicates your support without overstepping boundaries.

Consistency in spending quality time together is pivotal. It's not always about planned activities; sometimes, casual moments strengthen bonds. Create rituals unique to your relationship—a weekly coffee outing, cooking together, or evening strolls after dinner to look at the stars. These shared experiences become cherished touchstones, reinforcing the value you place on your relationship.

Always respect their individuality by valuing their opinions, even if they differ from yours. Foster open communication, establishing an environment where they feel comfortable expressing themselves without fear of judgment. This openness nurtures mutual respect and a deeper understanding of one another.

Patience is essential; friendships take time to evolve and deepen. Understand and respect their pace and preferences. Let the bond grow organically by consistently demonstrating authenticity, genuine interest, and care for their well-being and interests. Trust and understanding will gradually solidify, creating a resilient and sincere friendship, as well as a healthy marriage with your new spouse. They will be so proud of the relationship you are creating with their child.

Have a Yes Day

Implementing a "yes day" can be an enjoyable and impactful activity to strengthen your bond with your stepchild. During this designated day, you prioritize saying "yes" to any and all reasonable requests within predetermined boundaries. For instance, if they request to have a movie marathon, visit a museum, or try a new hobby, accommodating these requests within reasonable limits encourages their decision-making and fosters a sense of empowerment.

This experience provides an opportunity for mutual understanding where they learn the importance of responsible decision-making while feeling validated and heard. It also offers a chance to engage in activities they enjoy, fostering a sense of closeness and shared experiences between you and your stepchild.

Setting clear boundaries for the "yes day" ensures that both parties understand the limits of permissible requests. For example, agreeing to participate in outdoor activities but within a certain timeframe or budgetary constraints maintains a balance between fun and responsibility. This exercise not only allows them to feel in control but also demonstrates your willingness to engage in activities that interest them, fostering a more open and trusting relationship.

The "yes day" can result in memorable experiences that create lasting impressions. Whether it involves trying new cuisines, exploring a nearby nature reserve, or even just having a designated day filled with fun activities, this dedicated time strengthens your connection and builds positive associations, creating cherished memories for both you and your stepchild. If you're really lucky, maybe your stepchild will allow you to have your own yes day!

Encourage Them to Try New Things

Encouraging your stepchild to explore new activities is an opportunity to embark on an enriching and transformative journey together. Trying new things, whether it's a sport, a culinary adventure, or an artistic pursuit, can open doors to unexpected passions and discoveries. It's about fostering an environment that promotes curiosity, growth, and a willingness to step beyond familiar territories.

To initiate this journey, start by discussing various interests and activities with your stepchild. Listen attentively to their aspirations and desires, and gently introduce them to new possibilities that align with their interests. For instance, if they show an inclination towards outdoor activities, suggest exploring hiking trails, trying rock climbing, or even organizing a camping trip. The key is to present options that excite and resonate with their interests while gently nudging them toward new experiences.

Supporting their endeavor to try new activities involves more than just suggestions—it's about active participation. If they express an interest in a new hobby or skill, consider joining them in the learning process. For instance, if they're curious about photography, embark on photo walks together, exploring different perspectives and techniques. This not only shows support but also creates shared experiences that strengthen your bond.

Additionally, consider providing resources and opportunities for learning. Research classes or workshops that cater to their interests, or find local community groups where they can explore their newfound passions alongside peers. This guidance and encouragement offers reassurance and demonstrates your commitment to their growth and development.

Encouraging them to step out of their comfort zone also means fostering a mindset that embraces challenges and uncertainties. Celebrate their willingness to try new things, even if the outcomes aren't perfect. Emphasize the importance of the learning process itself rather than focusing solely on the results. This mindset shift helps them develop resilience, adaptability, and a willingness to embrace change—a crucial aspect of personal growth and development as a lifelong learner.

Creating an environment that celebrates exploration and new experiences is pivotal. It fosters a sense of curiosity, adaptability, and a willingness to take risks—a set of invaluable traits for navigating life's challenges. Ultimately, the journey of trying new things together isn't just about discovering new hobbies; it's about nurturing a mindset that embraces growth, resilience, and the joy of discovering one's capabilities and passions.

Maintain a Sense of Humor

Infusing humor into your interactions with your stepchild can significantly enhance the family dynamic. You don't need to be a comedian to infuse some healthy humor into daily life! Sharing lighthearted moments or engaging in playful banter creates a comfortable and enjoyable atmosphere that fosters closeness. For example, sharing funny anecdotes from your own experiences or enjoying a good-natured joke together during meals or outings can uplift everyone's spirits and create lasting memories.

Humor acts as a bonding agent, bringing people together and strengthening connections. Incorporating laughter and lightness into daily interactions can diffuse tension, ease stressful situations, and create a sense of unity. Whether it's teasing each other playfully or sharing a humorous story, these moments not only break the ice but also foster an environment where everyone feels more relaxed and at ease.

Learning about someone else's sense of humor can be a delightful endeavor, but it often requires a nuanced approach to avoid potential awkwardness. Observing and understanding what makes your stepchild laugh without forcing the humor can set the stage for more organic and enjoyable interactions.

Start by observing their reactions to different types of humor in casual settings. Notice their responses to jokes, TV shows, movies, or memes, and pay attention to what kind of humor they naturally gravitate toward. For instance, if they enjoy witty wordplay or slapstick humor, take note and consider incorporating similar elements into your interactions. Maybe it's time to bust out your old *Three Stooges* DVDs!

When engaging in humor, begin with light-hearted and universally relatable jokes or stories. This can be as simple as sharing amusing anecdotes from your own experiences that aren't too personal or potentially embarrassing. For example, recounting a funny mishap during a family trip or a comical incident from your childhood can help break the ice without making anyone uncomfortable.

Another approach is to gently test the waters by sharing jokes or memes that are popular or widely appreciated. This allows you to gauge their reactions without delving into more personal or potentially sensitive humor. Pay attention to their responses—do they laugh or smile? If they seem engaged, it might indicate a similar taste in humor. This can be a beautiful thing!

As conversations flow, gradually introduce light humor into everyday interactions. This could be through playful banter or teasing, but always maintain sensitivity to their comfort level and boundaries. A self-deprecating joke about a minor mishap or a harmless pun during a shared activity can create a relaxed atmosphere without feeling forced or awkward.

Additionally, be open to embracing their sense of humor and showing appreciation for it. Laugh along with them when they share something funny or acknowledge their wit and humor, reinforcing a positive atmosphere and validating their comedic style. Never laugh at them.

However, it's essential to be mindful and avoid sensitive topics, offensive humor, or jokes that could potentially be hurtful. Humor is subjective, and what's funny to one person might not resonate with another. If in doubt, err on the side of caution and keep humor light, inclusive, and respectful.

Ultimately, learning about someone else's sense of humor is a gradual process that evolves through shared experiences and mutual understanding. It's about creating an environment where laughter feels natural and enjoyable for everyone involved, contributing to a warm and harmonious family atmosphere.

Utilizing humor also showcases your approachability and relatability. By sharing jokes or finding amusement in everyday situations, you're demonstrating that you're someone they can comfortably engage with and confide in. This shared laughter creates shared experiences and helps forge a stronger, more positive relationship, allowing you and your stepchild to connect on a deeper level beyond the roles of parent and child.

Finally, humor can act as a powerful tool to navigate through challenges. It's not about making light of serious situations but finding moments of joy and levity amid life's ups and downs. Encouraging laughter and playfulness within the family dynamic cultivates a warm and welcoming environment, contributing to a more enjoyable and connected household. The lightness of laughter can sometimes lift a heavy heart.

Play With Your Stepchild

Engaging in playful activities with your stepchild, regardless of their age, remains an exceptional way to foster a deeper bond and create meaningful memories that transcend time. From elementary school to high school, adapting playful interactions to suit their changing interests and maturity levels is key to maintaining that connection. As they grow older, their preferences may evolve, so it's crucial to approach these activities with their current interests in mind.

If you find yourself with a stepchild who is younger than school-aged, pretty much any activity is centered around play because that is how our youngest learners acquire knowledge. The use of STEM toys, books, outside time, and blocks are great places to start. Show them at an early age that learning does not need to be stoic or overly academic to be impactful.

For elementary school-aged children, activities like building Lego sets, exploring nature on a hike, or even concocting science experiments at home can be both educational and entertaining. For instance, creating a mini herb garden together not only introduces them to gardening but also provides an opportunity for shared responsibility and the joy of watching something grow. Engaging in these activities shows your interest in their world and encourages a sense of exploration and curiosity.

As children enter their preteen and early teenage years, their interests might gravitate toward more complex board games, outdoor adventures like kayaking or rock climbing, or engaging in creative DIY projects. This might involve more advanced crafting, like building a birdhouse, creating digital art, or even learning a new musical instrument together. For instance, embarking on a photography expedition can be a fantastic way to explore their burgeoning interests while creating memorable snapshots of shared experiences.

The essence of these playful activities isn't just the specific task at hand but the shared enthusiasm and quality time spent together. Whether it's a basketball match, experimenting in the kitchen with a new recipe, or engaging in a game of chess, these moments allow for laughter, relaxation, and genuine connection. They create spaces where both you and your stepchild can unwind and authentically be yourselves.

Playful interactions offer more than just bonding moments; they serve as invaluable teaching moments. Through play, children of any age learn essential life skills like problem-solving, communication, and resilience. For instance, collaborating on a complex puzzle or engaging in strategy games sharpens their critical thinking and decision-making abilities. It's not just about the activity itself; it's about the shared experience and the lessons ingrained within.

Moreover, as children transition into adolescence, these playful engagements provide a gateway for open communication. Whether it's discussing life experiences while painting together or sharing thoughts during a shared hike, these relaxed settings often lead to more candid conversations, allowing you to understand their perspectives and concerns more intimately.

Ultimately, the key is to remain adaptable and open to exploring a variety of activities that align with their interests and developmental stage. These playful interactions transcend mere fun; they reinforce trust, respect, and a sense of camaraderie. They're the building blocks of a harmonious family dynamic that continues to evolve and flourish over time. So pick up that pickleball racket and head over to the court!

Share Their Enthusiasm

Celebrating your stepchild's achievements is a continuous journey that greatly influences the atmosphere within your blended family. It's more than recognizing milestones; it's about nurturing an environment where accomplishments, no matter how big or small, are embraced and acknowledged. Acknowledging academic triumphs, personal victories, or instances of self-discovery contributes to a positive and encouraging atmosphere. For example, if they demonstrate exceptional effort on a test or excel in mastering a new skill, showcasing genuine pride and enthusiasm for their achievements highlights your recognition of their dedication and hard work.

Moreover, actively participating in their excitement further strengthens your bond. If your stepchild is thrilled about a hobby, interest, or achievement, engaging wholeheartedly in their joy by celebrating together can create delightful and lasting memories. It could involve arranging a small gathering, organizing a family outing, or simply enjoying a special meal to commemorate their success. This shared celebration not only validates their emotions but also solidifies the connection between you both, creating a sense of unity and belonging. You are doing things *together*.

However, acknowledging their excitement or accomplishments doesn't solely revolve around significant events; it extends to embracing daily victories or moments of happiness. For instance, if they express enthusiasm about a book they're reading, taking the time to discuss the storyline or characters with genuine interest showcases your support for their passions. These seemingly small yet thoughtful gestures of acknowledgment and celebration affirm their feelings and encourage ongoing open communication.

Through shared enthusiasm and celebration, you're cultivating more than just recognition of their accomplishments; you're nurturing a positive atmosphere where their successes are embraced and celebrated regularly. This ongoing support and recognition fosters an environment of encouragement and validation. It builds their confidence, reinforcing the idea that their efforts and achievements, no matter the scale, are valued and appreciated within the family setting.

Additionally, encouraging them to set goals and offering support in their pursuit of these aspirations further cements your commitment to their growth and development. Be an active listener when they discuss their aspirations; offer guidance and assistance as needed; or connect them with resources if you are not the best outlet. For instance, if they express a desire to improve in a particular subject, offering resources or scheduling dedicated study sessions conveys your investment in their ambitions. This proactive support not only celebrates their current achievements but also encourages them to aim higher and persist in their endeavors.

Furthermore, tangibly showcasing their achievements reinforces their sense of pride and accomplishment. Displaying their artwork, certificates, or awards in a prominent place at home communicates your admiration for their hard work and dedication. It's a constant reminder of their capabilities and the value you place on their achievements, fostering a sense of pride and validation.

Above all, ensure that celebrations are not just about the end result but also about the effort and dedication put forth. Encourage a growth mindset by emphasizing the importance of resilience, perseverance, and learning from setbacks. Highlighting the journey toward success rather than just the outcome instills valuable lessons and fosters a culture of continuous improvement and personal growth.

Create Family Traditions

Family traditions are an integral part of fostering a sense of unity and belonging within a blended family. These rituals create a shared history, providing moments of connection and stability while honoring and holding space for the past. For instance, initiating a weekly movie night where everyone takes turns picking the film or a monthly family game day builds anticipation and excitement, marking it as a cherished tradition.

Annual traditions like a camping trip or a family vacation hold significant value by creating lasting memories and reinforcing the family bond. Planning an annual getaway where everyone participates in the decision-making process of the destination or activities establishes a sense of togetherness and collective enjoyment.

Moreover, holiday traditions can be particularly impactful. Creating and nurturing holiday traditions in a blended family is a beautiful way to weave a tapestry of togetherness and shared experiences. Picture a scenario where your newly blended family comes together during the festive season. To establish a cherished tradition, you decide on a "Secret Santa" gift exchange where everyone draws a name and anonymously gifts a thoughtful present. The anticipation and surprise add an element of excitement, making it a treasured event woven into your family's holiday tradition.

In addition to this, the act of decorating the house together becomes an annual ritual. It's not just about putting up the tree and stringing lights;

it's about the laughter, shared stories, and moments of connection that come with it. Each ornament placed on the tree carries a memory or a story, building a shared history that becomes an integral part of your family's narrative.

Cooking and sharing special meals during holidays are also traditions that transcend generations. In a blended family, these moments hold a unique significance. Imagine the kitchen bustling with activity as family members gather to prepare a meal together, each contributing their favorite dish. These shared culinary experiences don't just create delectable feasts; they weave a tapestry of flavors that signify unity, love, and the joy of coming together.

Engaging in charitable activities as a family during holidays is another impactful tradition. It could involve volunteering at a local shelter, organizing a food drive, or participating in community service projects together. These acts of kindness and giving back not only instill valuable lessons in empathy and compassion but also strengthen the family bond by collectively contributing to the well-being of others.

Establishing these traditions isn't merely about following a routine; it's about creating a shared culture and identity. It's about weaving threads of unity and stability within your family tapestry while respecting all that has brought them to this moment with your family. The predictability and familiarity of these rituals offer a sense of comfort and security, especially during times of transition or change. They create a framework for shared experiences, strengthening the bond among family members and nurturing a sense of belonging and togetherness.

Furthermore, involving everyone in the decision-making process when planning these traditions fosters inclusivity and reinforces the notion that everyone's voice and preferences are valued. Suppose your family plans an annual camping trip during the summer. In that case, allowing each member to suggest activities or destinations ensures that everyone feels part of the tradition, fostering excitement and anticipation for the upcoming adventure.

These traditions become the cornerstone of your family's identity, embracing the uniqueness of each member while celebrating the collective spirit that binds you all together. They're not just moments on the calendar; they're milestones in your family's journey, carrying with them the warmth of shared experiences and the joy of creating lasting memories.

Through these traditions, families can reinforce their bond, instill values, and offer a sense of predictability and security, providing a framework for shared experiences that contribute to a harmonious and connected family unit. You are both your own people and a family.

Make New Memories Together

Creating new memories is a wonderful way to deepen connections within a blended family. If you have been heeding the advice outlined in this book, memories are part of the fun and will arise out of this process. Embarking on adventures together, such as a weekend getaway to a nearby town or planning a DIY home project, offers opportunities for shared experiences and bonding. Embarking on joint projects serves as an incredible way to solidify the bonds within a blended family. Engaging in DIY home projects or shared hobbies can create a lasting impact on relationships. Consider activities like building a birdhouse, crafting homemade decorations, or refurbishing furniture together. These ventures not only encourage teamwork but also cultivate an environment where creativity and collaboration flourish.

For instance, imagine the joy of working on a DIY home improvement project alongside your stepchild, whether it's revamping a room's decor, constructing a backyard garden shed, or building a treehouse. The shared effort, problem-solving, and sheer delight of bringing a project to life can deepen the connection between you and your stepchild. Such endeavors offer a unique space for shared accomplishments and a sense of pride in the collective creation.

DIY projects provide a fantastic platform for learning and skill development. For example, assembling a piece of furniture or working on a car repair project not only fosters camaraderie but also offers opportunities to share knowledge and learn together. It's a chance to impart practical skills while reinforcing the bond between a stepparent and stepchild.

Moreover, these projects offer a canvas for self-expression and creativity. Consider painting a mural together or constructing a family photo collage. Such creative endeavors not only enhance the aesthetic appeal of your home but also serve as a tangible representation of the collective effort and shared experiences within the family. These projects serve as visual reminders of unity and collaboration, reinforcing the bond among family members.

The key to successful DIY projects is not just the outcome but the process itself. Embrace the imperfections, enjoy the laughter, and celebrate the milestones achieved together. It's less about the final product and more about the shared experience, the moments of learning, and the sense of accomplishment that strengthen the connection between a stepparent and stepchild. Through DIY projects, you build more than just tangible items; you construct lasting memories and forge deeper, meaningful connections that contribute to the fabric of your family.

Engaging in activities that cater to everyone's interests and preferences is a powerful way to ensure inclusivity and enjoyment within a blended family. Consider spending a day at a local amusement park where everyone can choose a ride or activity that excites them. Organizing a family sports tournament, whether it's basketball, soccer, or even a mini-golf competition, can spark friendly competition and laughter. Even a themed family costume day, when everyone dresses up according to a chosen theme, can turn into a day filled with joy and shared moments of creativity.

Celebrating milestones together, whether significant achievements or smaller victories, strengthens the family bond. Acknowledging accomplishments in academics, sports, or personal milestones like birthdays and anniversaries fosters a sense of recognition and support within the family unit. These celebrations become more than mere events; they are opportunities to affirm each other's successes and reinforce the idea that every member's achievements are valued and celebrated.

The essence of these shared experiences lies not just in the event itself but in the connections forged during these moments. They serve as building blocks for a shared narrative within the family. Each experience, whether it's a thrilling day at an amusement park or a heartfelt celebration of achievements, contributes to the family's story, creating a tapestry of memories that binds members together.

To make these moments more impactful, consider involving everyone in the planning process: this cannot be highlighted enough in this book. Always listen first! Encourage each family member to contribute ideas for outings, celebrations, or themed days. This inclusive approach ensures that everyone feels heard and valued, fostering a sense of ownership and unity within the family.

Moreover, use these shared experiences as opportunities for open communication and bonding. Reflect on the day's events or celebrate milestones by sharing stories, discussing challenges, and expressing gratitude for each other's presence. These moments of reflection deepen the connections formed during these experiences and create a stronger sense of togetherness. Take pictures, jot down thoughts in diaries, save ticket stubs in special boxes, or create a time capsule each year to capture the events you've shared.

Remember that the value of these shared experiences extends beyond the event itself; it's about the laughter, the conversations, and the joy shared during these moments. They become the fabric of your family's history, shaping the bonds and relationships among members. Embrace these moments wholeheartedly, cherish the memories created, and nurture the unity and togetherness within your blended family.

Chapter Eight

Final Thoughts

Alyssa and Alison's Story

Once upon a time in the quaint town of Falmouth, MA, there lived a spirited stepdaughter named Alison and her stepmom, Alyssa. Their journey to forming a close bond was a delightful adventure filled with laughter, understanding, and a sprinkle of serendipity.

Alison was a vivacious teenager with a love for art and adventure while navigating the tumultuous waters of adolescence. Alyssa, her stepmom, was a kind and patient soul who had a passion for gardening and a knack for turning everyday moments into cherished memories. She had always wanted a daughter of her own, but fate had dealt different cards for her.

Their story began when Alison's father, Mark, and Alyssa decided to blend their lives into one big, beautiful family in their mid-forties. At first, Alison and Alyssa were like two puzzle pieces struggling to fit together. Alyssa, with her gentle smile and warm heart, recognized the challenge and decided to embark on a quest to unlock the key to Alison's heart. Alyssa remembered all too well how hard it was to fit in at her age.

One summer, after several months of living together without much progress in their relationship, Alyssa proposed a spontaneous road trip to an art festival in Western Massachusetts. The air buzzed with excitement as they strolled through vibrant booths, hand in hand, exploring various artworks. Alyssa, determined to connect with Alison through her love for art, suggested they try painting a mural together in one of the activity areas. As paintbrushes swirled and laughter echoed, a masterpiece of memories was created. Alyssa and Alison found their thing!

As Alyssa talked about her green thumb on the way home, their journey continued with Alyssa introducing Alison to the world of gardening when they came home. Initially skeptical, Alison soon discovered the therapeutic magic of planting seeds and watching them bloom into beautiful flowers. In a way, it was like art. Together, they transformed the backyard into a colorful oasis, their hands covered in soil and hearts intertwined. Many of the fragrant blooms they planted still come back each year, no matter how much time has passed.

One chilly winter evening, Alyssa surprised Alison with a cozy movie night. As they snuggled under blankets, Alyssa shared stories of her own teenage years, fostering a sense of understanding between them. Alison, in turn, confided in Alyssa about her dreams, fears, and the complexities of being a teenager in a blended family. Alison's mother had never been truly present for her in all the ways that Alyssa was able to be—while never replacing her mother, who had moved abroad for the military the summer Alyssa moved in.

As the years passed, Alison and Alyssa became inseparable. From impromptu dance parties in the living room to heartfelt conversations over cups of hot cocoa when Alison came home from college for long weekends, their connection deepened. Alyssa's patience and love helped Alison navigate the challenges of adolescence, while Alison's energy and enthusiasm brought new life to Alyssa's world. As adults, they are now more friends than stepchild and stepparent, but such is life. All children grow up.

Their journey is a testament to the power of love, patience, and the magic that happens when two souls decide to embark on a shared adventure in keeping with our tenets of learning to love your stepchild. It is not always easy, but it will not always be hard. Alison and Alyssa had not only become family but also the closest of friends, forever grateful for the beautiful tapestry they had woven together. Often they can be seen on Old Silver Beach on their matching beach chairs, sipping iced tea and talking about everything and nothing.

Where to Go From Here

Embracing stepchildren as cherished, respected, and loved family members irrespective of blood ties is pivotal in fostering an enduring and supportive relationship. The evolution of the concept of family extends far beyond biological connections, emphasizing the significance of emotional bonds, care, and mutual respect. You have found yourself in a place where you can honor your pasts and look forward to your connected futures. In a world where relationships are no longer solely defined by lineage, acknowledging and treating stepchildren as genuine family members stand at the heart of nurturing a loving relationship.

The traditional notion of family has been redefined throughout time and individually to your own unit. You define your family. Stepparents stepping into the lives of their partner's children often encounter unique challenges and opportunities. However, treating stepchildren with love, empathy, and a genuine sense of belonging sets the stage for building strong relationships that you will hold in your heart forever.

Acknowledging the inherent worth of stepchildren within the family dynamic is instrumental in creating an environment of acceptance and support. That is where it starts. Each individual brings a unique set of experiences and strengths, and recognizing and celebrating these differences is key to fostering a loving relationship. Treating stepchildren as true family members involves actively participating in their lives, showing interest in their activities, and offering guidance and support. Therein lies the beauty!

This evolution of family structures has brought forth a realization that love and care are not confined by biological relations. It's about the emotional bonds and the dedication to nurturing and supporting each other. Stepparents embracing this understanding and considering their stepchildren as valued members of the family lay the foundation for meaningful and affectionate relationships.

Inspirational stories abound that highlight the transformative power of treating stepchildren as genuine family members. Narratives of stepparents going above and beyond, not out of obligation but out of love and genuine care, demonstrate the immense impact of embracing stepchildren as true family. These stories resonate with the essence of what family truly means—love, understanding, and unwavering support irrespective of blood ties.

The significance of treating stepchildren as genuine family members lies in the creation of a safe and nurturing environment. This environment allows stepchildren to express themselves freely, seek guidance, and form deep emotional connections. It's about building relationships based on trust, respect, and compassion, where stepchildren feel acknowledged, valued, and supported.

The expanded nature of family to include those unrelated by blood exemplifies the beauty of diverse connections. Families are now defined by the strength of their bonds rather than biological ties alone. This inclusivity and acceptance paves the way for stepchildren to feel a sense of belonging and security within the family unit.

Moreover, treating stepchildren as true family members contributes to their emotional well-being and development. Research has shown that strong emotional connections and a sense of belonging within a family positively impact children's self-esteem, mental health, and overall happiness. By embracing stepchildren as integral parts of the family, stepparents play a pivotal role in their emotional growth and resilience.

Treating stepchildren as true family members is a testament to the expanding definition of family—a definition founded on love, empathy, and mutual respect. Embracing stepchildren with open hearts and minds, acknowledging their worth, and actively participating in their lives lays the groundwork for fostering loving and enduring relationships. As the concept of family continues to evolve, it underscores the beauty and strength of connections forged not only by blood but also by love, care, and acceptance.

Embracing the journey of loving a stepchild involves traversing a path that extends far beyond the traditional familial roles. It's an endeavor that speaks volumes about your commitment to embrace a family dynamic founded on love, understanding, and compassion. This journey typically commences at the juncture where you intertwine your life with someone who already holds a profound place for their child or children from a prior relationship. Congratulations on embarking on this profound commitment—a testament to your willingness to embrace the complexities of blended family life.

Recognizing this endeavor as a transformative journey is key. It transcends conventional familial boundaries, challenging predefined roles and societal norms. It's an exploration of love that is diverse and boundless. This kind of love signifies an amalgamation of hearts and souls where genuine connections are woven, nurtured, and treasured. Your choice to actively engage with resources like this book signifies not just a commitment but a dedication to understanding, learning, and evolving within this unique familial dynamic.

The profound depth of this bond can't be understated. It's a testament to the limitless capacity for love, empathy, and growth. Engaging in this relationship goes beyond nurturing a child's emotional well-being. It becomes a catalyst for personal evolution, fostering growth, empathy, and resilience within yourself. The endeavor to love a stepchild actively cultivates connections that extend beyond the immediate present, shaping the fabric of relationships that last a lifetime.

This journey often starts with an intricate interweaving of hearts and experiences. You step into a realm where the traditional notion of family expands, where love is redefined through shared experiences, celebrations, and challenges. It's an opportunity to embrace the beauty of differences, celebrate the uniqueness of each family member, and acknowledge the tapestry of individual stories that form the collective narrative of your blended family.

Embracing this journey of loving a stepchild opens a door to profound growth and understanding. It's about navigating through the complexities of relationships, embracing moments of joy, learning from challenges, and celebrating milestones together. Each step taken in nurturing this bond contributes not just to the well-being of the child but also to the transformation and enrichment of your own life, creating connections that resonate through the echoes of time.

Imagine a scenario where a stepfather, Jack, wholeheartedly embraces his role in his new blended family. He understands that nurturing a stepchild isn't just about fulfilling a role; it's about creating a nurturing environment. By fostering emotional security, acceptance, and unwavering support,

Jack creates a safe space for his stepchild, Anna, to blossom. Through shared interests, they create a unique bond that surpasses the confines of traditional parent-child relationships. Jack's journey involves continual self-reflection, challenging his beliefs about parenting and relationships. This introspection fuels his personal development, cultivating patience and resilience not just for himself but for Anna as well.

In another instance, Sarah, a stepmother, navigates the complexities of bonding with her stepson, Max. Understanding Max's unique personality traits becomes her compass. Through shared experiences and acknowledging Max's individuality, Sarah forges a bond that surpasses the boundaries of blood relations. Their shared memories become the foundation of an enduring connection, creating a cohesive family unit that celebrates unity and togetherness. This journey, while challenging at times, teaches Sarah adaptability and resilience, virtues she passes on to Max through grace and understanding. Remember that while it may not always be perfect, your family is yours and no one else's. Stay strong, and the rest will come!

Loving a stepchild is akin to planting seeds that blossom into an evergreen legacy. The rewards burgeon far beyond fleeting moments of satisfaction; they flourish into an enduring sense of contentment that permeates every facet of life. Consider the intangible treasures that a committed stepparent imparts—a legacy woven with threads of empathy, understanding, and boundless love. This heritage becomes a guiding beacon for forthcoming generations, instilling a blueprint for love, acceptance, and compassion within the family tapestry. Individuals like Jack and Sarah, who wholeheartedly embrace their roles in blended families, undergo a profound metamorphosis shaped by these experiences, redefining their perceptions of love, relationships, and the very essence of family.

The significance of loving a stepchild transcends the immediacy of the present; it blooms into a legacy that reverberates through generations. It's a transformative journey that unfurls new horizons, nurturing personal growth and forging connections that surpass the conventional confines of family. Within this expedition, though strewn with its share of challenges, lie invaluable moments of joy, shared laughter, and poignant life lessons. Each laugh echoes, and each lesson learned etches an indelible mark on the hearts of those intertwined in this loving relationship. Loving a stepchild isn't merely an act; it's an embodiment of courage, compassion, and resilience that bequeaths rewards transcending temporal and personal boundaries.

The legacy of loving a stepchild extends far beyond individual fulfillment. It shapes a lineage of understanding and kindness, rewriting the familial narrative for generations to come. It sets forth a paradigm where love isn't bound by biological ties but flourishes in the fertile soil of empathy and connection. The experiences, challenges, and triumphs woven into this journey create a rich tapestry of memories—a legacy that doesn't merely fade with time but rather becomes the cornerstone of the family's collective history.

Within this intricate tapestry lies the beauty of metamorphosis. As individuals like Jack and Sarah walk this path, they undergo profound transformations, their characters sculpted by empathy, fortitude, and love. Their perspectives on relationships evolve, their understanding of love deepens, and the essence of family undergoes a renaissance. Through the challenges and triumphs, they pave the way for a legacy defined not by bloodlines but by the strength of the bonds forged through shared experiences and unwavering affection.

Loving a stepchild isn't immune to challenges. It requires courage to navigate uncharted territories, resilience to weather storms, and compassion to understand the intricacies of evolving relationships. Yet, within these challenges lie the seeds of growth and resilience. It's an ongoing odyssey, a testament to the enduring power of love that transcends time, nurturing enduring connections that etch themselves into the annals of familial history.

Throughout the extensive journey of this guide, we've ventured into the depths of three distinct archetypes: the introspective Cave Dweller (CD), the expressive Mountain Yeller (MY), and the adaptable Straddler, who embodies a fusion of these traits. Understanding these archetypes is pivotal, as they intricately mold the dynamics within relationships. We intended to furnish you with a rich assortment of tools not only to fortify connections with others but notably to facilitate introspective growth. As you delve into insights about your own nature, you inherently become a more valuable presence for others, including your stepchild.

Empowered by the wisdom gleaned from these chapters, you now possess a unique lens to not only interpret actions but also discern motivations with heightened clarity. Brace yourself for a paradigm shift as you begin to see your stepchild—and perhaps even yourself—from a radically new perspective, one that considers the nuances of personality archetypes and the spectrum of human behavior.

Our expedition through these chapters has been a revelatory odyssey into the foundational attributes of CDs, MYs, and Straddlers, honoring the intricacies intrinsic to each persona. Unraveling these distinctions endows you with the ability to decode your stepchild's actions within the framework of their individuality. This skill is an invaluable tool, circumventing assumptions that often fuel toxic environments and unwarranted conflicts.

Imagine the scenario of Sarah, a stepmother embracing the insights from this exploration. Sarah recognizes her stepdaughter's inclination toward introversion, aligning with the traits of a Cave Dweller. Understanding this, Sarah adapts her approach, offering space for her stepdaughter to express herself at her own pace. This adjustment helps foster trust and comfort, nurturing a deeper connection between them.

Similarly, imagine Jack, a stepfather, encountering his stepson's boisterous nature, reminiscent of a MY with some Straddler tendencies. Armed with the understanding gained from these archetypes, Jack navigates this with grace, finding ways to engage positively with his stepson's expressive personality in spite of his reserved nature. He constructs an environment where his stepson feels heard and valued, laying the groundwork for a harmonious relationship based on both of their needs and ways of communication.

Understanding these archetypes isn't just about decoding behavior; it's a transformative tool for building bridges of understanding and empathy. It's about respecting the uniqueness of each individual, avoiding the traps of assumptions, and fostering environments that nurture understanding and respect. Applied with care, these insights hold the potential to transform relationships, guiding them toward deeper understanding, acceptance, and enduring connection.

Relationship conflicts and misunderstandings are commonly attributed to a lack of love, empathy, or respect. More often than not, these stem from misunderstanding rather than a dearth of affection. Failing to recognize the inherent personality traits guiding your stepchild's actions risks misinterpreting their intentions, leading to unwarranted tension. Instead, by acknowledging and respecting these inherent differences, we foster greater empathy, allowing love to bloom fully and nurture an enduring relationship.

Engaging with the principles of *50 Ways to Love Your Stepchild* isn't a quick fix but a commitment to an ongoing journey that can improve just about every other area of your life, too, with the right application. Love, in its true essence, demands consistent attention, persistent effort, and a willingness to evolve. This guide serves as a compass, offering invaluable guidance, but the real application resides in your actions and dedication. It's about embracing love as a process, not merely a destination.

As you delve into the material, expect moments that challenge your preconceptions about parenting, relationships, and life itself. These instances of uncertainty or confusion aren't roadblocks but stepping stones toward genuine growth. Embracing these challenges is where the true essence of this journey lies. It's an opportunity to explore uncharted territories within yourself, fostering personal evolution and establishing deeper connections with your stepchild.

This journey isn't just about navigating the intricacies of stepparenting; it's a call for self-discovery. Each step forward is an opportunity to understand yourself better: to recognize your strengths, acknowledge your limitations, and grow from both. Relish this process of self-exploration. It's an integral part of nurturing a fulfilling relationship with your stepchild and evolving as an individual.

Please note that the essence of this journey extends beyond creating a connection with your stepchild; it's about reshaping your whole approach to relationships. Perhaps your own children! By dedicating yourself to understanding, patience, and resilience, you're not just enhancing one bond but fundamentally transforming the way you connect and interact with your loved ones. It's an opportunity to redefine what it means to be part of a family, creating an environment of mutual respect, empathy, and enduring love.

Embracing this journey isn't without its challenges; it demands commitment and persistence. Yet, within this commitment lies the seed of profound change. It's an investment that redefines your life's purpose, creating a legacy of love that spans generations. Every effort and every moment of dedication contributes to building a legacy of compassion, understanding, and love, leaving an indelible mark on the lives of those you hold dear.

It's not just about navigating the present; it's about shaping the future. As you embark on this journey, remember that it's the small, consistent steps of everyday life that forge enduring relationships with your stepchild, your spouse, and far beyond. Cherish the moments of growth, celebrate the milestones along with the heartache, and feel the deep connections that you are cultivating. Here's to the journey ahead—a journey filled with challenges, rewards, and the enduring legacy of love you're building for your family. Cheers to the transformative power of love and the bonds it forges! May the rest of your life begin...

Appendices

Self-Assessment Questionnaire: Determine whether You're a CD, MY, or Straddler.

In the quest for self-understanding, recognizing one's intrinsic personality traits plays a crucial role. This self-assessment questionnaire has been carefully designed to help you discern whether you align most closely with the introspective nature of a Cave Dweller (CD), the extroverted inclinations of a Mountain Yeller (MY), or the balanced characteristics of a Straddler. By reflecting on your behaviors, preferences, and reactions in various situations, this tool aims to provide insight into your predominant personality type. Approach each question with honesty and openness, and remember, there's no right or wrong answer—just a deeper understanding of your unique self waiting to be unveiled.

Personality Indicator #1

Circle one answer per question.

1. Have you ever walked in your sleep during your adult life?

YES or NO

2. As a teenager, did you feel comfortable expressing your feelings to one or both of your parents?

YES or NO

3. Do you tend to look directly into a person's eyes when talking to them?

YES or NO

4. Do you feel that most people, when you first meet them, are uncritical of your appearance?

YES or NO

5. In a group situation with people you've just met, would you feel comfortable drawing attention to yourself by initiating a conversation?

YES or NO

6. Do you feel comfortable holding hands or hugging someone you're in a relationship with in front of other people?

YES or NO

7. When someone talks about feeling warm physically, do you begin to feel warm also?

YES or NO

8. Do you tend to tune out when someone is talking to you because you're anxious to come up with your side of the story?

YES or NO

9. Do you feel that you learn better by seeing and/or reading than by hearing?

YES or NO

10. In a new class or company meeting, do you usually feel comfortable asking questions in front of the group?

YES or NO

11. When expressing your ideas, do you find it important to relate all the details leading up to the subject so the other person can understand it completely?

YES or NO

12. Do you enjoy relating to children?

YES or NO

13. Are you comfortable with your body movements when faced with unfamiliar people and circumstances?

YES or NO

14. Do you prefer reading fiction rather than non-fiction?

YES or NO

15. If you were to imagine sucking on a juicy lemon, would your mouth water?

YES or NO

16. Do you feel comfortable receiving a compliment in front of other people?

    YES or NO

17. Do you feel that you're a good conversationalist?

    YES or NO

18. Do you feel comfortable when complimentary attention is drawn to your physical body?

    YES or NO

Personality Indicator # 2

Circle one answer per question.

1. Have you ever awakened in the middle of the night and felt that you could not move your body and/or talk?

   YES or NO

2. As a child, did you feel you were more affected by your parents' tone of voice than by what they actually said?

   YES or NO

3. If someone you know talks about a fear that you've experienced before, do you tend to re-experience that apprehension or fear?

   YES or NO

4. After arguing with someone, do you tend to dwell on what you could or should have said

YES or NO

5. Do you tend to occasionally tune out when someone is talking to you and therefore don't hear what's being said because your mind drifts to something totally unrelated?

YES or NO

6. Do you sometimes desire to be complimented for a job well done, but feel embarrassed or uncomfortable when complimented?

YES or NO

7. Do you often fear not being able to carry on a conversation with someone you've just met?

YES or NO

8. Do you feel self-conscious when attention is drawn to your physical body or appearance?

YES or NO

9. If you had a choice, would you rather avoid being around children most of the time?

YES or NO

10. Do you feel uptight in body movements, especially when faced with unfamiliar people or circumstances?

YES or NO

11. Do you prefer reading non-fiction rather than fiction?

YES or NO

12. If someone describes a very bitter taste, do you have difficulty experiencing the physical feeling of that bitter taste?

YES or NO

13. Do you generally feel that you see yourself less favorably than others see you?

YES or NO

14. Do you tend to feel awkward or self-conscious holding hands and/or kissing someone you're in a relationship with in front of other people?

YES or NO

15. In a new lecture or company meeting, do you usually feel uncomfortable asking questions in front of the group?

YES or NO

16. Do you feel uneasy if someone you've just met looks you directly in the eyes when talking to you, especially if the conversation is about you?

YES or NO

17. In a group situation with people you've just met, would you

feel uncomfortable drawing attention to yourself by initiating a conversation?

YES or NO

18. If you're in a relationship or are very close to someone, do you find it difficult or embarrassing to verbalize your love for them?

    YES or NO

Personality Indicator Scores

Personality Indicator #1

- Give yourself 10 points for every *yes* answer for questions one and two.

- Give yourself 5 points for every answer for questions three through eighteen.

- Write the total number at the top of #1's questionnaire.

Personality Indicator #2

- Give yourself 10 points for every *yes* answer for questions one and two.

- Give yourself 5 points for every answer for questions three through eighteen.

- Write the total number at the top of #2's questionnaire.

- Combine the total from the two Personality Indicators.

Using the Scoring Chart

On the scoring chart, look up the combined score of Personality Indicators 1 and 2 on the HORIZONTAL axis of the chart and circle the number.

- Take the total score of PI #1, locate it on the VERTICAL axis of the chart, and circle the number.

- Draw a horizontal line across the page from the PI 1 score; then draw a vertical line down from the combined score.

- The number in the box where the two lines intersect represents your true adjusted percentage personality indicator.

- Scores 61 and higher indicate a Mountain Yeller personality type.

- Scores 45 and lower indicate a Cave Dweller personality type.

- Scores 47 to 56 indicate a Straddler personality type.

Cave Dweller Tendencies

- Reserved
- Head-ruled
- Controlling
- Wants space and security
- Prefers socializing one-on-one
- Singular focus
- Thinks before reacting

- Prefers showing affection privately
- Distrusts flattery
- Enjoys working alone
- Enjoys individual activities
- Wants alone time
- Dresses for comfort
- Decides after thinking about it
- Speaks literally, to the point
- Infers from what others say
- Feels emotional pain in the mind
- Fears loss of security

Cave Dweller Priorities

- Career/Financial Security
- Hobbies/Children
- Relationships/Family
- Sex/Lovers

Mountain Yeller Tendencies

- Outgoing

- Heart-ruled
- Dominating
- Wants connection and touch
- Enjoys socializing in groups
- Moving focus
- Reacts spontaneously
- Comfortable with affection anytime
- Likes reassurance and compliments
- Enjoys working with people
- Enjoys team activities
- Wants to be together as much as possible
- Decides in the moment
- Speaks inferentially—adds story
- Takes what others say literally
- Feels emotional pain in body and mind
- Fears rejection

Mountain Yeller Priorities

- Relationships/Sex
- Family/Children

- Friends/Hobbies

- Career/Financial security

SCORE # 1

0	5	10	15	20	25	30	35	40	45	50	55	60	65	70	75	80	85	90	95	100	COMBINED SCORE #1 AND #2
0	10	20	30	40	50	60	70	80	90	100											50
0	9	18	27	36	45	55	64	73	82	91	100										55
0	8	17	25	33	42	50	58	67	75	83	92	100									60
0	8	15	23	31	38	46	54	62	69	77	85	92	100								65
0	7	14	21	29	36	43	50	57	64	71	79	86	93	100							70
0	7	13	20	27	33	40	47	53	60	67	73	80	87	93	100						75
0	6	13	19	25	31	38	44	50	56	63	69	75	81	88	94	100					80
0	6	12	18	24	29	35	41	47	53	59	65	71	76	82	88	94	100				85
0	6	11	17	22	28	33	39	44	50	56	61	67	72	78	83	89	94	100			90
0	5	11	16	21	26	32	37	42	47	53	58	63	68	74	79	84	89	95	100		95
0	5	10	15	20	25	30	35	40	45	50	55	60	65	70	75	80	85	90	95	100	100
0	5	10	14	19	24	29	33	38	43	48	52	57	62	67	71	76	81	86	90	95	105
0	5	9	14	18	23	27	32	36	41	45	50	55	59	64	68	73	77	82	86	91	110
0	4	9	13	17	22	26	30	35	39	43	48	52	57	61	65	70	74	78	83	87	115
0	4	8	13	17	21	25	29	33	38	42	46	50	54	58	63	67	71	75	79	83	120
0	4	8	12	16	20	24	28	32	36	40	44	48	52	56	60	64	68	72	76	80	125
0	4	8	12	15	19	23	27	31	35	38	42	46	50	54	58	62	65	69	73	77	130
0	4	7	11	15	19	22	26	30	33	37	41	44	48	52	56	59	63	67	70	74	135
0	4	7	11	14	18	21	25	29	32	36	39	43	46	50	54	57	61	64	68	71	140
0	3	7	10	14	17	21	24	28	31	34	38	41	45	48	52	55	59	62	66	69	145
0	3	7	10	13	17	20	23	27	30	33	37	40	43	47	50	53	57	60	63	67	150
0	3	6	10	13	16	19	23	26	29	32	35	39	42	45	48	52	55	58	61	65	155
0	3	6	9	13	16	19	22	25	28	31	34	38	41	44	47	50	53	56	59	63	160
0	3	6	9	12	15	18	21	24	27	30	33	36	39	42	45	48	52	55	58	61	165
0	3	6	9	12	15	18	21	24	26	29	32	35	38	41	44	47	50	53	56	59	170
0	3	6	9	11	14	17	20	23	26	29	31	34	37	40	43	46	49	51	54	57	175
0	3	6	8	11	14	17	19	22	25	28	31	33	36	39	42	44	47	50	53	56	180
0	3	5	8	11	14	16	19	22	24	27	30	32	35	38	41	43	46	49	51	54	185
0	3	5	8	11	13	16	18	21	24	26	29	32	34	37	39	42	45	47	50	53	190
0	3	5	8	10	13	15	18	21	23	26	28	31	33	36	38	41	44	46	49	51	195
0	3	5	8	10	13	15	18	20	23	25	28	30	33	35	38	40	43	45	48	50	200

About the Author

Dr. Cline lives with her husband, two daughters, two German Shepherds, and two Yorkies in the hills of North Carolina. Her expertise in relationship-building has offered her the opportunity to travel around the world as a keynote speaker and international workshop facilitator.

www.ingramcontent.com/pod-product-compliance
Lightning Source LLC
Chambersburg PA
CBHW070110080526
44586CB00013B/1257